COSMIC CARE

Astrology, Lunar Cycles, and Birth
Charts for Self-Care and Empowerment

VALERIE TEJEDA

HAY HOUSE, INC.
Carlsbad, California • New York City
London • Sydney • New Delhi

Published in the United States by: Hay House, Inc.: www.hayhouse.com
Published in Australia by: Hay House Australia Pty. Ltd.: www.hayhouse.com.au
Published in the United Kingdom by: Hay House UK, Ltd.: www.hayhouse.co.uk
Published in India by: Hay House Publishers India: www.hayhouse.co.in

Cover design: Kathleen Lynch
Interior design: Claudine Mansour Design

Cataloging-in-Publication Data is on file at the Library of Congress

Tradepaper ISBN: 978-1-4019-7450-3
E-book ISBN: 978-1-4019-7451-0
Audiobook ISBN: 978-1-4019-7452-7

10 9 8 7 6 5 4 3 2 1
1st edition, February 2024
Printed in the United States of America

COSMIC CARE

*To the bookstores that helped my teenage self
discover astrology books—thank you!*

CONTENTS

Introduction   xi

Chapter 1   ARIES   1

Chapter 2   TAURUS   15

Chapter 3   GEMINI   29

Chapter 4   CANCER   41

Chapter 5   LEO   55

Chapter 6   VIRGO   69

Chapter 7   LIBRA   83

Chapter 8   SCORPIO   97

Chapter 9   SAGITTARIUS   111

Chapter 10 CAPRICORN   123

Chapter 11 AQUARIUS   137

Chapter 12 PISCES   151

Chapter 13 LUNAR CYCLES   165

Chapter 14 BIRTH CHARTS   185

Conclusion   201

Appendix 1: Equinoxes and Solstices   203

Appendix 2: How to Set the Energy in Your Space   211

Acknowledgments   215

About the Author   217

Do you ever gaze at the sky and see something bright?
And get mesmerized by its beautiful light?
And get lost in dreaming about your life?
And then lock those dreams away?

Have you forgotten that you are allowed to be happy?
Have you forgotten that you are deserving of joy?
Have you forgotten that you are worthy of love?
Maybe you haven't forgotten, but you just need
a reminder.

You have the power of the sun,
the brightness of the stars,
and the light of the moon,
all within you.
You are made of stardust and brimming with magic.

Come, let's remind you.

INTRODUCTION

There's something magical about being in tune with the energy around you—with the natural cycles in nature, with all the seasons and phases of our lives.

You may even have noticed that during certain times of year, you feel a specific energy in the air. Maybe you feel happy and rejuvenated by the fresh flowers of spring, or maybe you feel playful during the heart of summer. When the first leaves start to fall in autumn, maybe you feel like cooking your favorite meal or reading your favorite book, and once winter rolls around, you feel contemplative and reflective during the cold, dark days. The wheel of the year charms us during every season, and it aligns with all twelve zodiac signs.

Astrology is a great tool for understanding ourselves and the universe, and tapping into its energy. It is the language of the stars and is the study of time, energy, and celestial patterns, but essentially, it's just one big calendar based on thousands of years of observational research (for example, that when the sun, moon, or planets are in certain positions, there are certain themes associated with the event). But the planets and luminaries do not control outcomes. Astrology is correlation, not causation.

The astrological wheel moves us through an entire year around the sun, and the lunar cycle is the roughly 29.5

days of moon phases that move us through each month. Both the sun and the moon take us from one point in time to another: from a beginning and to an end.

Within this astrological calendar, there's a story: the journey from Aries to Pisces, which is full of archetypes that we all can glean lessons and inspiration from.

In addition, we each have a specific moment in time when we entered this world, and this magical moment of ours gives us each a birth chart—our own individual cosmic map to help inspire us along our own journey.

Since the beginning of civilization, people have looked to the stars and planets for guidance. It's natural for us to want to live in harmony with the cosmos—it's ingrained in our DNA. This is how our ancestors lived, and that's why living in tune with the astrological seasons and moon phases—and taking it a step further by looking at our birth charts—can often lead to more of a sense of peace and harmony in our lives. It can be incredibly motivating and encouraging as well.

Astrology can help you to feel seen. It does *not* define you, but what it can do is help to confirm your intuition and natural gifts and help you to see potential in certain areas in your life. It is *not* meant to put you in a box, but rather to help you identify things about yourself. Because, while we're all made of the same stardust, we each still have our own unique magic.

I think we all can agree that we want to feel our best— that we all want to feel loved, happy, safe, accepted, and valued; that we want to be taken care of and have our needs met. At the end of the day, we all desire peace, love, and happiness—it's just that we often don't think we deserve them.

I know I didn't. For so long, I thought I wasn't worthy of being happy, that I wasn't worthy of (or even able to have) peace in my life, and that the pain I was feeling was just part of my existence—a curse I had to live with, if you will.

But once I started valuing myself and believing I was worthy of joy, a lot of things began to change in my life. I was able to heal through the pain, find my peace, and cultivate happiness in my life. Astrology played a role in that.

When it comes to astrology, my saying is: "The cosmos can inspire our lives, but it does not control our lives. *We* are the authors of our story." Astrology gives us this great cosmic map, a guide to help us connect with the different parts of ourselves and to the energy around us, but *we* decide how to read the map. It's not a belief system; it's a tool.

When I tell people that astrology has played a huge role in my personal growth, I'm sometimes met with confused reactions. Many wonder, how can something like astrology help you discover more about yourself and grow as a person? Likely it's because when some think of astrology, what first comes to mind are pop horoscopes and memes. But the truth is, there's a whole world of astrology beyond those. You can use it to help attune to the seasons, the cycles of the moon, and the archetypes in your birth chart. Astrology can act as a tool for self-discovery.

I've spent most of my life trying to figure people out—myself included. This is why I was drawn to a degree in psychology and why I have certificates in astrology and music therapy. The desire to know is also what drew me to working as a journalist and writing books. I'm obsessed with knowing what makes people tick and understanding more about how they operate.

When I was 18, I used to go to the bookstore with a coffee in hand and headphones on, and I would roam the astrology section. It was one of my favorite things to do. I bought books on the topic often, because I wanted to learn as much as I could about it. This obsession continued into college.

Between my psychology classes, I would sneak away to the bookstore to read my books and dive even deeper into astrology. I have to tell you, I've loved every single minute of learning about it. Becoming an astrologer and an author of nonfiction and fiction books has been one of the most fulfilling parts of my life, and I feel incredibly grateful to be able to share this passion of mine with you.

Think of me as your older sister or auntie who just wants you to be happy and have the joy and peace you deserve. I just want you to look in the mirror and be so damn in love with yourself that no matter what's going on in this human experience (that is sometimes so lovely and sometimes so heartbreaking), you can be secure in your worth.

That's what this book is meant to do—help you find more peace and joy in your life and more love for yourself. I truly believe that gaining a greater understanding of the natural rhythms of the universe can help to remind you that you're a part of something bigger and greater, which can be comforting during life's more trying moments. It's also such a great way for us all to relate to each other.

THE SIGNS, STARS, AND SEASONS

Twelve constellations make up the zodiac—the constellations of stars along the *ecliptic*, the circle that the sun makes once a year as it travels around the planet.

So when I say "Libra season" or "the sun is in Libra," I'm referring to the sun's position in the Libra constellation.

In this book we'll go through all twelve zodiac signs and astrological seasons, their energy, and their well-being themes. We'll go over corresponding rituals, meditations, tarot cards, and tarot and oracle spreads; affirmations, element, ruling planet, and other things. For each sign, I offer recommendations for crystals that work best when you attach an affirmation to them that aligns with what each crystal represents—for example, you can connect with rose quartz using the affirmation "I am love." I also include herbs that correspond with the energy of each sign, but when considering ingesting or using herbs topically, please consult your doctor or medical practitioner for safety.

Each sign has multiple archetypes, lessons, and attributes that we can all get inspiration from, which is why each zodiac chapter is designed to be applicable to everybody, despite what your sun sign happens to be. And while you might connect more with certain zodiac energies over others, all can still serve a purpose when it comes to addressing personal needs. So, as you approach each astrology sign chapter, be open to seeing how it speaks to you. You never know which sign might surprise you.

Astrology is the language of the stars, and astrologers interpret this language differently. Know that this book is based on my interpretation and years of study—your interpretation and intuition may take you in a different direction. Remember also that astrology is by no means a perfect tool. Humans created astrology, and humans are not perfect. As you make your way through this book, take what resonates with you and leave what doesn't.

The idea is to take each well-being theme, lesson, and inspiration you get from every sign with you through the wheel of the year, starting with Aries—the sign that kicks off at the equinox and the astrological new year.

Just like the zodiac wheel is the journey around the sun from Aries to Pisces, we will be doing a year of inspiration from the signs to enhance our well-being.

From there, we go over the monthly phases of the moon to harmonize our lives with the magic of the lunar cycle. After that, we cover birth chart basics so you can level up, attuning to the astrological seasons and moon phases and learning more about yourself in the process.

While there are many different astrology systems out there, I am using Western astrology and the Northern Hemisphere for the seasonal symbolism in nature. However, if you're in the Southern Hemisphere, this book still applies to you! The symbolism, even if noted in the Northern Hemisphere, is for all of us to understand regardless of location.

In addition, wherever you are in your astrological journey, whether you're a beginner, a seasoned veteran, or a moderate astrology lover, there's something here for you too. This book is for all!

Now, before we dive into things, I want to add a little disclaimer here . . . as mentioned above, I believe astrology can greatly improve your life and have a huge impact on your well-being, helping with self-discovery and personal growth. But it's not a cure-all. It's not going to fix everything. None of the things we go over in this book are meant to replace medication, therapy, or other things a doctor or medical professional prescribes to improve your quality of life.

What I can say is, living in tune with astrology and the lunar cycles, and learning more about myself through my birth chart, assisted me in my growth and personal healing process. It was not the thing that healed me, but it *was* a piece that helped me feel more whole again.

This project comes from a place of love. I see you. And I'm grateful to have you along on this cosmic journey with me.

ARIES

Welcome to the astrological new year. There's something magical about a new beginning, a fresh start. It's about giving yourself a clean slate and beginning again, leaving the past behind. Aries season is the first sign in the zodiac wheel. And with it comes a new, fresh energy that we all can tap into and allow to inspire us.

In the Northern Hemisphere, Aries season lines up with spring and the vernal equinox. During this time, the birds are chirping, the flowers are blooming, the grass has turned to a luscious shade of green, and the days are starting to get longer and warmer. New life is budding all around. We see renewal, rejuvenation, things moving forward—the pure excitement and joy in just being alive. This metaphor in nature is one of the reasons why Aries season is a time of growth, renewal, and personal empowerment. The energy typically focuses on new beginnings, taking action, and independence.

Aries season (when the sun is in Aries) usually takes place from around March 21st through April 19th (the exact dates each year can be different by a day or so). If you were born during Aries season, your sun sign is Aries, and you came into this world with access to the powerful, forward-moving energy that Aries exudes.

Aries is a cardinal sign, which means it ushers in the beginning of a new season and initiates something. Its element is fire, and its elemental symbol is a spark. Aries, then, is the spark that births new beginnings, where life is created from nothing and where new ideas are formed. Aries energy is motivating and inspirational. Do you know that phrase, "light a fire under (someone)"? It means to encourage someone—or yourself—to move faster, to take action, to get things going. That's the fiery energy of Aries.

Like its symbol the Ram, Aries charges forward on instinct. Neither is afraid to leap before they look, to move with fearlessness, to strike while the iron is hot—or to welcome competition. They try new things and have new experiences.

The energy of Aries is bold, brave, enthusiastic, passionate, courageous, impulsive, and independent. An archetype associated with this sign is the Warrior. Aries is ruled by Mars, which is named after the Roman god of war. This gives Aries a fighting spirit. It doesn't mean those with Aries energy are out to pick a fight; just that they are not afraid to fight—especially for the things and people that they care about. They are a symbol of strength, courage, and leadership, which is why another archetype associated with the sign is the Hero.

Aries are natural leaders, but that doesn't mean they all necessarily *want* to be at the helm. This gift of leadership can also be expressed by encouraging others, hyping them up, and cheering them along the way. While they might have the reputation of being fighters, they are also fierce lovers and always extremely supportive of their own.

A driving trait behind those with Aries energy is deep passion. It can present in how they love, how they care for others, and how they want to see people bloom and blossom. It's a really good thing to have an Aries on your team.

Aries thrive at starting new endeavors, at getting projects off the ground. They tend to be self-starters, which is why there are so many Aries entrepreneurs. Not only are they talented at launching things, they can also get others excited about them and inspire support.

The flip side of thriving on newness, however, is that they don't often stick to one thing for the long haul. Aries can feel stifled if they go for too long without experiencing something new. They can often scratch that itch with something as simple as trying a new restaurant, a new activity, or even working in a field that's constantly changing. The newness doesn't always have to be something massive, but Aries do need novelty in their lives. They're also independent, which means they're comfortable acting for themselves (and not necessarily that they all like to be alone).

Aries are known for being competitive, but mostly, it's with themselves. With Aries, the biggest thing I've observed when it comes to competition is that they want to win—but this doesn't mean they don't want others to win too.

As I mentioned, Aries are natural cheerleaders, and they like to see people thrive. Your Aries friend will be in the front row at your basketball game, supporting you at your business launch, and dancing beside you at your birthday party. They will encourage you and give you all the high fives along the way. But if you sit down and play a game of chess with them, they'll want to beat you at least once, just to prove *to themselves* that they can.

Aries also likes to be the first to do something. At the root of this desire is their bravery and courageousness. They're not afraid to break down those walls and barriers to try a path that no one has ventured down before. This relates to another archetype I love that corresponds with Aries: the Pioneer. Aries will try new things, take a different route, and go where no one else has gone. They'll try something just to see how it works out. They appreciate the journey of it all, the adventure.

I'm a big music buff, and I see the strong Aries energy among some of the most legendary female vocalists in the music industry: Diana Ross, Mariah Carey, Aretha Franklin, Celine Dion, Chaka Khan, Selena Quintanilla Pérez, Lady Gaga . . . all these singers are Aries suns, and they're pioneers. They did things their own way and paved the path for many who followed them. They allowed their flames to burn bright, and they fearlessly and unapologetically put their art out in the world.

In addition, these singers were honest and vulnerable, and they exuded their love, passion, and heartbreak in their music. Many of them happen to be the voices behind some of the biggest love songs of our time. This shows once again how one of Aries' most admirable strengths is not only tapping into passions but also sharing them with the world.

Aries teaches us to follow our heart and to let our passion be our guide, to fight for what we believe in and take that risk—to try something we've never tried before. And if it doesn't work out, just shrug your shoulders, shake it off, and move on to something new, because that's what an Aries would do.

ARIES SEASON THEME

In addition to the archetypes and energy that correspond with each sign, there's a key phrase that shows the sign's integral values. Aries' key phrase inspires the direction our self-care takes during its season. The phrase is "I am."

Aries rules the first house of self in astrology. This house represents *you*, your likes, your dislikes, your self-interest, and your vitality. It's often considered the most personal of the astrological houses, since the spotlight is on you.

The focus that Aries puts on the self means the theme for Aries season centers around returning to ourselves, valuing ourselves, and putting ourselves first. Because that's what everything starts with—the self. If we don't take care of ourselves first, we won't have the energy we need to put into anything else. Aries understands that.

In our society, the relationship we have with putting ourselves first, especially as women, is difficult to manage. We're told we're supposed to be self-sacrificing, that our needs come last, and that we need to give and give and give without receiving.

But this is exactly the opposite of how it should be. We need to care about other people, of course. But the truth of the matter is, we can't pour from an empty cup. The greatest gift you can give to yourself is care, *and* it's also the greatest gift you can give to those you love and the world at large. When we feel good, when our energy is bright, we radiate that energy, which in turn helps the people around us feel good too. When we put our well-being first, we can be kinder, more compassionate, and more loving both to ourselves and those around us.

Looking back over my life, I can't even tell you how many times I wish I had put myself first. I see those experiences as teachable moments. For many years, I ran myself into the ground for a job or for other people around me, and it very much impacted my physical and mental health. This was because I didn't think I was allowed to put myself first, that I was worthy of such a thing. Once I realized how taking care of myself was of the utmost importance, putting my needs on the back burner was something I made a point to not let happen again.

When the sun is in Aries, it's a great reminder to prioritize ourselves and value our needs, to remember that they matter and that you matter. Putting ourselves first is the foundation of caring for our well-being, making this the perfect way to kick off the astrological year.

ARIES SEASON RITUAL

The ritual during Aries season focuses around prioritizing ourselves and our needs. A great way to get into the headspace for putting yourself first is to set your energy for the day, ideally in the morning, and you can pair this ritual with any other morning routines you have.

Begin by setting your space, if you wish (if you need some guidance or more ideas for this, please refer to the Appendix). Lighting candles in particular is a great way to connect with the fire energy of Aries. If you would like to work with crystals, color, or herbs for this ritual, see the Correspondence section below.

Take a few deep breaths in through your nose and out through your mouth. Then take a few more, and think about an intention you want to set for the day that centers around prioritizing your well-being. This could look something like taking a stroll outside, dedicating some time to journal or read, relaxing on the couch to watch your favorite TV show, or mapping out steps to reach a particular goal. Cement that intention mentally (words are spells). If you like, write it down in your journal, or jot it on a sticky note and put it somewhere you'll see it during the day.

After setting your intention, take a few more deep breaths and ponder how you can take action today to support your intention. Again, you can just focus on it mentally or write it down, whatever you prefer.

Then, take a moment to think of something about yourself that you're grateful for. Since the theme for Aries season is the self, make it about you. For example, I might say, "I am grateful that I'm patient and that I see the best in other people."

When you're ready, end the ritual by reminding yourself that you are valuable and that prioritizing yourself and your well-being is of the utmost importance.

ARIES SEASON MEDITATION

Here's a simple meditation you can do to connect with the energy of Aries season:

Find a quiet and comfortable place, free (as much as it can be) of distractions.

Take a few breaths in through your nose and out through your mouth. Allow your body to relax.

As you focus on your breath, pay attention to any areas in your body where there's discomfort or tension. As you breathe, imagine those areas relaxing and releasing the tension.

Now, bring your attention to your heart and imagine that there's a warm, glowing light surrounding it. As you continue to focus on this light, say the affirmations "I am worthy," "I am enough," "I am brave," and "I am allowed to prioritize myself."

After repeating the affirmations a few more times, with your attention still on that light around your heart, imagine how it feels to take care of yourself and prioritize your well-being without any guilt. Sit with that feeling for a little bit.

When you're ready, open your eyes and carry this feeling with you. You can return to it whenever you need.

Aries Season Affirmations

Here are some affirmations to connect to the energy of Aries season. If these affirmations don't resonate with you, feel free to adapt them to fit your needs while still channeling the passionate spirit of the Ram.

I am fearless.

I believe in myself.

I trust my instincts.

I am confident and courageous.

I am full of energy.

I am an unstoppable force, full of vitality and enthusiasm.

I take bold action toward the things I am passionate about.

I am capable of anything that I put my mind to.

Aries Season Journal Prompts

What excites me most about this new beginning and new season?

What can I add to my daily routine to help prioritize my well-being?

What are some things that I feel motivated by during this season?

What are some things about this cosmic fresh start that I'm grateful for?

What is one step I can take today to align with my intentions?

Aries Season Card Spread

This five-card tarot/oracle spread focuses on the energy of the sun in Aries. To do a card spread, shuffle the cards and fan them out in front of you, face down. Pick five cards that you feel most drawn to and use them for reflection with the questions below.

1. What is my main focus for Aries season?

2. What areas of my life may benefit from Aries energy?

3. What is something that's sprouting new growth in me this season?

4. What old patterns need to be burned away to make space for new growth?

5. What sparks of inspiration can I embrace to fuel my fire?

Crystals for Aries Season

Ruby inspires passion, vitality, and courage. You can use it to encourage determination and to inspire you to pursue your objectives with confidence and zeal.

Carnelian promotes passion and creativity. It aligns with Aries enthusiasm and can help spark inspiration.

Red jasper promotes protection, stability, and a sense of security. It promotes vigor and vitality by fostering your connection to the earth and to your physical body.

Fire agate promotes bravery, self-assurance, and endurance. Many believe it can strengthen willpower and resiliency as well as assist in overcoming difficulties and roadblocks.

Citrine crystals bring success, abundance, and good fortune. Citrine helps you to draw wealth, prosperity, and abundance into your life.

Herbs for Aries Season

Rosemary promotes clarity, focus, and positive energy. You can use it to strengthen your resolve and attention, as well as to stay energized and inspired.

Peppermint scent helps with easing tension. It can promote relaxation and add a calming element to the fiery sign.

Nettle can provide hydration, vitality, and stability. It can help strengthen your ties to the ground and to your physical body, and help you maintain your vigor and vitality.

Ginger is also linked to the fire element and promotes warmth, vigor, and digestive assistance. It helps to boost personal power and vitality.

Marigold brings joy, happiness, and protection. This herb can also assist in maintaining your optimism and good spirits in the face of difficulties.

ARIES CORRESPONDENCES

Planet: Mars. Mars stands for energy, drive, action, and passion. It's the planet of boldness and courage and is linked to the Warrior archetype. Mars is a symbol for our willingness to take initiative, pursue our objectives, and establish and uphold our personal limits. Additionally, it represents physical vigor, love, and sexuality. In a birth chart, Mars can reveal information about a person's drive and ambition, and how one takes action. It can also show a person's propensity for determination, conflict, aggression, and hostility. Mars is named after the Roman god of war, and so it is the planet of the fighter and warrior. Mars is the fuel to our fire, and fiery Mars gives Aries their intense self-starting energy and confidence.

Color: Red. Red is frequently linked to passion, vigor, love, and strength. Red is the color of fire and blood, which are representations of life, vigor, and strength in nature. According to color psychology, red is connected to the physical body and the senses. It also evokes feelings of elation, self-assurance, and anger.

Element: Fire. Enthusiasm, passion, warmth, zeal, inspiration, and leadership are all correlated with the fire element. Aries, Leo, and Sagittarius are fire signs and are characterized by their confidence, bravery, vigor, passion, and creativity. They are motivated by their aspirations and goals and possess a strong spirit of exploration and adventure. Fire signs have a strong sense of identity and an independent spirit. They're risk-takers and experimental by nature, and they bring a dynamic energy to any situation. Fire is a symbol of renewal and purification because it can burn away the old and make room for the new. Fire can bring light and warmth, which can be comforting and inspiring. It also can fuel others and help light one's path. We see the fire element expressed through Aries in their passion, enthusiasm, and quick-moving nature.

Modality: Cardinal. In astrology, modalities show us how the signs operate and reveal the role they play in the astrological calendar to help move us through the year. Cardinal signs always initiate new seasons. Aries, as a cardinal sign and the first sign in the zodiac, initiates action and represents a new beginning.

Symbol: The Ram. The ram is a strong, stately animal renowned for its endurance, agility, and strength. It stands for bravery and tenacity and has represented strength and leadership throughout history. Aries are known for butting their "horns" up against any barrier until it crumbles. The ram is also a symbol of fertility and abundance, and it represents the affinity that Aries have for the fire element as well as their spirit of passion, inventiveness, and renewal.

House: First House of Self. The first house in astrology is the house of the self and the ego, and it's connected with the sign of Aries. It's a representation of you, including your likes, dislikes, self-interest, and vitality, and it symbolizes your sense of identity, how you present yourself to others, and how you act. It's linked to the traits of assertiveness, courage, and determination. The first house of a birth chart also stands for bodily well-being, vitality, and health, and it can also reveal information about a person's sense of self and their level of confidence and self-esteem. Additionally, it might reveal a person's aptitude for assertiveness and leadership as well as their capacity for goal setting.

Polarity Sign: Libra. Aries and Libra are the relational axis in astrology that looks at our relationships to our self and to others. Aries, a fire sign, is known for courage, tenacity, zeal, spontaneity, and an ability to take the lead. Libra, an air sign, connects to the virtues of harmony, balance, and fairness. Libras are renowned for their charisma, diplomatic skills, and their appreciation of harmony, beauty, and the arts. Aries and Libra are complementary elements that balance each other. While Libra offers grace and diplomacy, Aries gives passion and energy. Aries can teach us lessons on how to love ourselves, while Libra can teach us lessons on how to love others.

Tarot Card: The Emperor. The Emperor card corresponds with Aries and represents power, steadiness, and authority. The Emperor is a strong and dominating figure who has traits like bravery, tenacity, and assertiveness. He acts as a prompt to take command of your life and claim your power.

TAURUS

We now move from the new beginning—the passionate and action-oriented season of Aries—to the grounding, pleasureful, and present energy of Taurus. New life is birthed through Aries, and life is maintained and sustained through Taurus. While Aries is quick and fast-moving, Taurus is slow-moving and steady. The energy shifts toward laying down roots; cultivating, maintaining, and enjoying what's around us; and being present and finding happiness in all of life's pleasures.

Taurus is ruled by the second house of abundance and material things. This doesn't mean that a Taurus is shallow and cares only about material items—quite the contrary. They just know how to appreciate and enjoy all things in life. They are experts at taking their time to savor and slow down, whether it be while eating a beautiful meal, spending time with loved ones, or just taking in the beauty of nature. Tauruses are great at making the most of each and every moment.

Tauruses enjoy being comfortable. They're the type who eats dessert before dinner (if that's what they're craving). They'll put work aside if there's an opportunity to play, or take a longer vacation if they need it. They enjoy indulging and unwinding. Living a rich, fulfilling existence is what this sign's energy is about. When Tauruses find something they like, something that brings them enjoyment, they want to experience it over and over and over. It wouldn't be unusual for a Taurus to eat the same thing every day for lunch and also have an album they've been listening to on repeat for the last few years.

Just as they like to enjoy, they want those around them to feel good too. They are *huge* advocates and supporters of those they care about. Moving and need help packing your apartment? Your Taurus friend will be there with the bubble wrap, and they'll bring the snacks and drinks, too. Taurus is that friend you can spend hours just talking to and feel comfortable enough to just be yourself with. They nourish those around them.

Taurus is an earth sign, connected to nature, and its elemental symbol is a lush field of grass that provides sustenance to others. Another Taurean elemental symbol is the earth's soil—the foundation in which life can flourish and grow.

From around April 20th to May 20th, the sun is in Taurus, and you have a Taurus sun sign if you were born during Taurus season. Taurus is the second sign of the zodiac calendar and is a fixed sign. Fixed signs are the essence of whatever season they are in. In the Northern Hemisphere, Taurus is the essence of spring. During this time, everything is in full bloom. Beauty is all around, and happiness is in the air. The planet Venus rules this sign, which couldn't be more appropriate given that

Venus is all about beauty, pleasure, connecting to the senses, and also abundance and prosperity.

Taurus energy is dependable, sensual, steadfast, prosperous, nurturing, strong, consistent, and romantic. Its symbol is the Bull, which speaks to the Taurean's stubborn, immovable nature. When a Taurus has their mind set on something, there's absolutely no way you're going to change it. And if they want to achieve something, they absolutely will.

Whenever I think of Tauruses, someone who often comes to mind is Cher. Cher is a pop music icon and total Taurus queen. Her big Taurus energy showed through in her 1996 interview with Jane Pauley when she shared a conversation between her and her mother: "My mom said to me, 'You know, sweetheart, one day you should settle down and marry a rich man. I said, 'Mom, I am a rich man.'" This empowering statement was about how she supported herself and didn't need anyone else to do that for her. And that's the thing about Tauruses: if they want something, they will make it happen—they don't need anyone to do it for them, and pretty much nothing will stand in their way.

This is one reason why Tauruses are known for being stubborn. And while stubbornness may carry some negative connotations, there are positive aspects to it as well—like being stubborn about working toward your dream, standing up for what you believe in, or making time for your well-being.

This stubbornness is one of Tauruses' greatest strengths and why many find success in life—but it's based on *their own* definition of success. For one Taurus, it could look like climbing the corporate ladder, and for another, it could be living in a country cottage, tending to their own lush garden. Regardless of what success looks like for them, they often achieve it.

Some archetypes associated with the sign are the Lover, the Sensualist, and the Builder. In fact, the key phrase for Taurus is "I build." The Builder is one of my favorite archetypes for the sign, because they're an energy that cultivates and cares for the land to ensure survival for themselves and those they love. Essentially, they want to make the world around them a pleasant one that they enjoy living in.

You could say that in a way, Taurus is an earth sign that teaches us how to do life on Earth, showing us the beauty of just enjoying the world before us. And that's something to admire about Taurus energy.

TAURUS SEASON THEME

Something I love about Taurus energy is how it can be so grounded in the present moment and the ability to savor what's before them. We see this in its symbol, the Bull, who is fully engaged and invested as he grazes and enjoys the green, lush grass, moving at his own pace and not distracted by external influences. This is why the theme we'll focus on for Taurus season is presentness and finding pockets of peace in the present moment.

Being present is not always easy. It might come more easily to Tauruses, but for many, it takes practice and work. So when the sun is in Taurus, it's a great time to hone this skill and harness this energy.

So many of us spend a lot of time absent from the present. It's so easy to do. We often focus on something that happened in the past, or we worry about the future. But the reality is: all that's truly guaranteed to us is the moment we're in, right here, right now. This is why being mindful and trying to find a sense of peace in each moment is so important.

But what if your present moment is not so good? What if you're going through a hard time? Just like the moon, our lives are always going to wax and wane. We'll have some good moments, and we'll have some bad ones. If you are currently going through a tough spot, I am genuinely sorry, and I send you lots of love. As I mentioned at the beginning of the book, astrology and getting in tune with the wheel of the year is not a cure-all, but it might help you find some peace in the midst of life's more difficult moments.

Being present and mindful, and engaging in things that bring you peace, can be especially helpful when times are tough. Let's say you're going through a stressful season, and something you really enjoy is reading, or watching your favorite film. Setting aside some time to be fully present while reading that book or watching that movie can offer a nice reprieve. It sounds simple, but in these times, it's often difficult even to plan time for ourselves.

I remember once in my life when I was really going through it. My health wasn't great, money was tight, I had a lot of anxiety, and it felt like everything seemed to be working against me. But one morning, I found an old gift card for a coffee shop. So I went and got myself some iced coffee and a pastry, and I sat outside in the sunlight to enjoy them. In the midst of my very chaotic world, I closed my eyes, took some deep breaths, and felt the sun against my face. I took the time to really savor my coffee and pastry (a delicious maple scone).

Did being present and enjoying that moment solve my problems? Did it make them go away? Absolutely not. But finding that little moment of peace helped keep me afloat that day. I truly believe that being able to ground yourself and find those pockets of peace in the present is a self-care superpower.

For me personally, a few things always bring me back to the present whenever my mind wanders in a different direction. I'm fortunate to live in an area in California where I have access to some beautiful trails, so I love doing mindful walks where I note the color of the sky and the trees I pass. I pay attention to the sound of the birds chirping and greet the people and dogs on the trail. A mindful walk is one of my favorite moments in my day.

But the truth is, you can turn just about anything into a mindful and grounding practice—drinking coffee (I give a coffee or tea ritual below), playing music or singing, cooking, reading a book, a TV show, a yoga class, playing chess, putting on makeup, a skin care routine, pulling some tarot or oracle cards . . . so many moments throughout the day can offer present, grounding, and peaceful practices if you look for them.

That's the thing about Tauruses—they're so good at finding those moments, all those little moments, and turning them into opportunities for enjoyment. And that's something that can inspire us all. When the sun is in Taurus, take it as a reminder to find those pockets of peace in the present and carry that tool with you throughout the year.

TAURUS SEASON RITUAL

This ritual focuses on mindfulness and enjoying the moment before you. You'll need a warm beverage, like a hot cup of coffee, tea, chai, or other drink of your choice. Preparing the drink can be part of the mindfulness act of the ritual as well, especially if you're creating a beverage that takes significant preparation, like matcha. If you're looking for an herb that aligns with Taurus energy to steep for tea, check the herbs section in this chapter.

After preparing your warm drink of choice, find a quiet place to sit with little to no distraction. With your drink in your hands, close your eyes and take a couple of deep breaths in through your nose and out through your mouth. With each breath, allow the tension to release from your body.

With your eyes still closed, notice how the drink smells as you take in another long, deep breath. What does it smell like? Earthy? Sweet? Notice the pleasant aroma as you continue to breathe.

With your eyes still closed, move your focus to your hands. What does the mug feel like against your palms and fingers? Is it nice and warm on your skin? Is the cup light or heavy?

Now open your eyes and gaze at your drink before you. What color is it? Are there lots of colors swirling in the cup? Do you notice any steam moving off the top?

As you take your first sip, bring your attention to the heat of the drink in your mouth. Feel the warmth of it and notice any sensations that you feel in your body after taking a sip.

Now, on your next sip, move your focus to how your drink tastes. Are you tasting any sugar that you put in it, or cream, or notes of a specific flavor? Is it enjoyable?

And as you continue to drink your drink, pay attention to all those things—the temperature of the drink, the flavor, how it feels in your body, and what it smells like as you continue to take breaths. And if your mind starts to wander, no need to judge that—just bring it back to these basic mindful things as you enjoy your beverage.

When you're nearing the end of your drink, recite to yourself, "I am grounded, I am peaceful, I am abundant, and I am grateful for this pause in my day." Carry that intention with you for the rest of your day.

TAURUS SEASON MEDITATION

Here's a grounding meditation to connect with the earth element of Taurus season energy:

Start by finding a peaceful, cozy area where you can sit or lie down. Close your eyes. Take a few slow, deep breaths in through your nose and out through your mouth, concentrating on how the breath feels as it enters and exits your body.

As you continue to breathe, visualize tree roots growing from the bottoms of your feet, going into the ground, and connecting you to the earth.

Now picture a tree in front of you. What does it look like? Notice its tall branches, strong trunk, and luscious leaves. See the roots of the tree going deep into the soil, anchoring it firmly into the ground. Notice the connection between the tree and the earth.

Now imagine your own roots merging with the roots of the tree, anchoring you and grounding you even further into the earth. And as you continue to breathe, feel that sense of calm and stability that comes from being grounded in nature.

When you're ready, open your eyes and return to the present moment. Carry that calm and grounded energy with you throughout the rest of your day.

Taurus Season Affirmations

Here are some affirmations to connect to the energy of Taurus season. If these affirmations don't resonate with you, feel free to adapt them to fit your needs.

I create environments that sustain me and provide for my needs.

I have faith in my own steadiness.

I work patiently toward my objectives.

Because I deserve prosperity, prosperity is drawn to me.

I feel a connection to the cycles of nature.

I appreciate all the joys in my life.

I'm willing to both give and receive love.

I am at peace, and I cultivate peace in my life.

Taurus Season Journal Prompts

What about Taurus resonates the most with me? Is there a lesson I can learn from the sign?

What aspects of my life need to become more stable, and how can I help them do so?

What are some basic pleasures I can enjoy and appreciate now?

How can being more patient and present in my daily life promote my well-being?

What self-care rituals can I include in my daily life, and how will they benefit me?

Taurus Season Card Spread

This five-card tarot/oracle spread focuses on the energy of the sun in Taurus. To do a card spread, shuffle the cards and fan them out in front of you, face down. Then pick five cards that you feel most drawn to and use them for reflection with the questions below.

1. How does the energy of the Taurus season impact me?

2. In what areas of my life am I ready for stability and progress, and how can I encourage this growth?

3. What assets do I have this season in terms of strengths and resources?

4. By embracing the energy of the Taurus season, what potential results or growth might I attain?

5. For me, which Taurus season feature is the most nourishing and nurturing?

Crystals for Taurus Season

Rose quartz represents love, compassion, and emotional healing. It can support your connection to your emotions and help you focus on love and self-love.

Malachite promotes balance, development, and transformation. It can assist you in your journey of development and transformation, and especially in letting go of unwanted thought patterns.

Amazonite is linked to expression, honesty, and communication. It assists in communication and self-expression and helps encourage you to share your thoughts and ideas with others.

Rhodonite promotes self-love, forgiveness, and compassion. It encourages us to take care of and foster love for ourselves.

Green aventurine represents luck, abundance, and success. It can help with attracting abundance, prosperity, and cultivating a growth mindset.

Herbs for Taurus Season

Lavender increases peace, relaxation, and clarity. It can provide a sense of security and grounding. It can also help with unwinding and letting go of tension.

Chamomile promotes harmony, calm, and emotional balance and can help with relaxation.

Rose stands for love, beauty, and sensuality. It helps with cultivating feelings of love and self-love and supports our relationship to our senses.

Nettle is connected to the earth element and provides hydration, vigor, and stability. It can increase vitality and fosters connection to the soil and to the physical body.

Passionflower is known for its calming and relaxing effects. It helps you find balance and cultivate inner peace.

TAURUS CORRESPONDENCES

Planet: Venus. Venus is the planet of love, beauty, harmony, values, and abundance. It's associated with the qualities of grace, charm, and diplomacy. This planet governs art and aesthetics as well as romance, partnerships, and relationships. Venus is also about enjoying pleasures, material comforts, and all of life's luxuries. Archetypes for the planet are the Lover, the Empress, and the Goddess. Tauruses express the Venus nature through their desire for comfort, seeking pleasure in life, and enjoying their peace.

Color: Green. The color green is often associated with harmony, peace, and abundance. Since green is the hue of plants and trees in nature, it's also connected with life and growth. Green, the color of healing, is known for being soothing. It helps release tension and stress. It's also connected to wealth and prosperity and is the color of good luck.

Element: Earth. The earth element represents stability, growth, practicality, safety, and rootedness. It symbolizes the foundation upon which all other things are built and the essence of the physical and material realm. Earth signs are known for being the builders of the zodiac. They are connected to the world around them. They are great at enacting plans to cultivate what they wish for in life. They enjoy routine and security. And just like the earth, they are strong and prosperous. We see the earth element expressed through Tauruses in their stability, groundedness, and consistency.

Modality: Fixed. In astrology, modalities show us how the signs operate and the role they play in the astrological calendar to help move us through the year. Fixed signs help stabilize the season and are the pillar and essence of the season they are in. Taurus, being a fixed sign, helps to cultivate and sustain the world around it.

Symbol: The Bull. The Bull represents the Taurus sign's affinity for the earth and the tangible world as well as their resolve and goal-oriented nature. Like bulls, Tauruses are strong, durable, and powerful. Bulls are renowned for their love of the physical world and delight in the senses as well as their commitment and steadiness. This aligns with Taurus's strong will and physical fortitude.

House: Second House of Abundance. The second house is the house of abundance, material things, and values and is ruled by Taurus. This house deals with money, belongings, and security. The second house is also about the way we value ourselves, and can help to reveal how we acquire, use, and manage our resources. It's also about what we need to feel comfortable and stable. The second house can shed light on how material conditions affect our sense of security.

Polarity Sign: Scorpio. Taurus and Scorpio—both fixed signs—are the growth axis in astrology. Scorpio is about what we need to let die to transform and grow, and Taurus is about how to flourish and blossom with all the new growth. This axis is also about resources: for Taurus, personal resources; and for Scorpio, the resources of others. As an earth sign, Taurus is characterized by solidity, realism, and a sense of foundation. Taureans are known for their appreciation of the physical environment and sensual pleasures. On the other hand, Scorpio is a water sign and is linked to traits like emotion, intuition, and metamorphosis. Scorpios are notable for their intensity, passion, and depth of feeling; for their capacity for change and evolution; and for their inquisitive nature. These energies can work together to foster positive development and change. Taurus is about shaping things, while Scorpio is about shape-shifting things. Taurus can teach us lessons on growth, while Scorpio can teach us lessons on transformation.

Tarot Card: The Hierophant. This card is frequently linked to conventional beliefs, organizations, and ideals. It can stand for instruction, learning, and the search for knowledge. The Hierophant is also about the necessity of conformity and abiding by set laws and conventions, as well as the significance of choosing a spiritual or philosophical path that speaks to you personally. The Hierophant can act as a prompt to explore fresh perspectives. Additionally, it can imply that now is a good time to look for spiritual or educational possibilities, or to get involved with a group or tradition that can offer support and direction.

GEMINI

We now move from the grounding, pleasureful, and present energy of Taurus season to the adaptable, playful, and communicative energy of Gemini season. While Taurus prefers to stay in one place and doesn't like to be rushed, Gemini is quicker and doesn't like to be tied down. Taurus is about consistency; Gemini, about versatility.

Gemini, the third sign, is an air sign—making this the first time we're introduced to the air element in the zodiac wheel. An elemental symbol for Gemini is clouds, as they are constantly moving and morphing and changing. They are the shape-shifters, the magicians, the storytellers. They are the jacks-of-all-trades and like to learn about a variety of things. They can be as unpredictable as the weather, and they like to keep people on their toes and express what's on their minds. They were born to communicate, and whether that's via writing, teaching, public speaking, broadcasting, or something else, they have a natural knack for dispensing information.

Like their symbol, the Twins, Geminis represent the duality in life and of the mind. They are good at nurturing all the different sides of themselves and expressing them all. They like to play all the parts. If a Gemini were in a film, they wouldn't just want to be the lead actor but also part of production, set design, scriptwriting, or even the makeup and costume team. They like to acquire new skills, which is why many Geminis are able to do a lot of things.

With the different sides they have, they love to gather new information. This can look like reading books, listening to podcasts, taking courses, or staying up to date on what's going on in the world. Information helps feed them, and they're incredibly curious about all things. They never stop asking questions and seeking answers; they are lifelong students.

The sun is in Gemini from about May 21st to June 21st. If you were born during Gemini season, then Gemini is your sun sign. It's a mutable air sign, and in the Northern Hemisphere, it transitions us as the last hurrah of spring before we welcome summer. It's like the end of the school year, and everyone's excited to move on to something new.

Like their polarity sign, Sagittarius, they also enjoy new experiences and feel bogged down by the mundane. But they can scratch the itch for newness by learning or discovering new things, which is why many Geminis are prominent readers and collectors of fun facts. They're the type of person you can just end up conversing with for hours on a variety of subjects. You're unlikely to find yourself running out of things to talk about when you're chatting with a Gemini.

Geminis are also talented researchers. Let's say you're traveling with one and want to go to a specific museum.

The Gemini will most likely research it beforehand and tell you all about it while you're walking through. They might even find a better museum to try and want to take you to that one too.

Adaptability—being able to move through life and handle whatever it throws at us—is also a Gemini strength. They don't get too bent out of shape if their plans change; they just find something else to do.

The energy of Gemini is versatile, inquisitive, witty, cerebral, playful, multifaceted, intellectual, adaptable, and communicative. Their planetary ruler is Mercury, which symbolizes communication and intellect. Their key phrase is "I think," speaking to their cerebral nature. An archetype that goes along with Gemini is the Messenger, because as mentioned, communication is their thing.

Connection is also a big part of Gemini energy. They need to feel connected to others. And regardless of how they connect, they still desire to connect with others in a way that they are comfortable with.

Geminis are also known for having a charm to them, but theirs is a bit different from that of, let's say, Libra and Leo, who are known for having strong charming energy. Gemini's charm comes with their play on words, their wittiness, and their ability to adapt to the room they're in; they are skilled chameleons. This skill is due to their ability to hold multiple identities at once, each authentic to who they are.

They're also known for being persuasive and cunning, which is why another archetype for the sign is the Trickster. They're good at taking opportunities and using them to their advantage. (Use this trait wisely, Geminis!) They can be incredibly convincing as well. One saying goes, "A Gemini could sell a wand to wizard," which is why, in addition to communicative fields, a lot of Geminis can find themselves in sales or marketing.

But one of my favorite things about Gemini energy is their ability to be in touch with all their different sides. Geminis aren't usually attached to a specific version of themselves. They're okay with their many sides and versions. Don't be surprised if one day, you meet your Gemini friend for coffee and she shows up with short, pink hair, a change from the long, blond hair she had the day before—or if your Gemini friend who's been in law school decides to go a different direction, pursuing art and nurturing their creative side. This can also look like having an incredibly eclectic book collection with topics from all across the board, or several completely different projects just to keep things interesting, or a wide variety of friends.

Geminis are also not afraid to change their opinion or stance on something, which sets them apart from the sign that precedes them—Taurus—which is known for more immovable opinions. Geminis are okay with changing their minds.

I have a brother who's a Gemini, and one of my favorite things about him is his ability to change his mind about something if you give him a valid reason. He will listen and consider all sides, and if new information brings him to a new conclusion, he will change his opinion. Gemini excels at this, being open to learning and understanding that opinions can—and sometimes should—change.

GEMINI SEASON THEME

For our Gemini season theme, we pull inspiration from this air sign's ability to change and move like the clouds. It's a great time to focus on the art of embracing changes in our lives and within ourselves.

Gemini is all about embracing one's many different sides and adapting and changing as one moves through life. It reminds us that it's okay to change and evolve and to nurture and love all the different parts of ourselves, and also to allow ourselves to grow as life around us changes. Because the reality is, the only constant in life is change.

When it comes to taking care of our well-being, accepting all the changes that life brings us is a truly fantastic tool. Even though many people dread or fear change, it can be a beneficial thing.

Change can allow you to learn new things, attempt new activities, and step out of your comfort zone. It increases your adaptability and readiness for everything life may throw at you—not to mention the benefits of developing your creativity when presented with new opportunities. While change can bring stress, it also makes you a better problem solver. In addition, the act of accepting change can improve your mental health by lowering stress and worry. Finally, it can aid in your personal development by raising your levels of self-awareness, self-compassion, and self-esteem.

Of course, there will be times in life when we experience incredibly hard and maybe even heartbreaking change. Change might not always feel exciting. But when we're left with no other option, adapting to the change we're presented with can help us keep our heads above water.

Personally, I've found the most peace in my life through acceptance—of myself, of other people, or of a situation. Acceptance can sometimes be the thing that helps to carry us through. I've had some exciting changes in my life and some that have been scary and difficult. But the biggest thing I've learned is to be kind to myself through all of life's changes and to try to find peace in the midst of it all.

Another part of embracing change for our well-being is giving ourselves permission to change, grow, and evolve. I've changed a lot over the last few years, and that's exciting to me—so much so, that often when I see old videos or photos of myself, I think, "Who is that person?" My opinions have changed, my perspectives have changed; even ways in which I like to spend my free time have changed. I'm grateful for that change in my life, and I want to keep evolving and growing.

While you're in Gemini season, see it as a reminder to embrace the change in your life and as an opportunity to play with the different sides of yourself. Remember: it's okay to change. Life is full of changes, just like the sign of the Twins, and all we can do is keep adapting.

GEMINI SEASON RITUAL

This ritual focuses on embracing the different sides of yourself and allowing yourself to express them.

For this ritual, you need a journal or paper and a pen, or you can type out your responses on a phone or tablet.

To begin, find a quiet place. To create a peaceful ambience, you could light a candle, burn some incense, turn on some soothing music, or set your space in other ways that make you feel comfortable and relaxed.

Take a few deep breaths in through your nose and out through your mouth. Focus on your breathing, consciously trying to clear your mind and release any tension in your body.

Next, take your journal and think about a side of yourself that you like but that doesn't get expressed often. For example, maybe you have a spontaneous side that you like, but you don't often do things that are very spontaneous. Whatever it may be, write it down. If more than one thing comes to mind, write them all down.

Now expand on what it would look like if you *embraced* that side of yourself. Using the example above, you would write what it would look like right now if you embraced your spontaneous side. You would describe what you would do, where you would go, how you would feel.

Once you're finished writing, read back what you wrote. While you're reading it, really take note of how you're feeling. Are you excited? Curious? Happy? Write down those feelings.

You're going to follow that by writing down the following affirmations:

I am allowed to embrace all the different sides of myself.

It is never too late to embrace another side of myself.

I am embracing more things that foster joy.

Feel free to add any more affirmations that come to mind and resonate with you.

When you're ready, close your journal, take a few deep breaths, and sit with how you're feeling. If this practice inspired you to embrace another part of yourself, follow that inspiration, and enjoy yourself in the process.

GEMINI SEASON MEDITATION

Here's a meditation to connect with the changeable nature of Gemini season energy:

Begin by getting into a comfortable position, whether sitting with your feet firmly on the ground and your spine straight, or lying down. Close your eyes. Take a few slow, deep breaths in through your nose and out through your mouth, and concentrate on how the breath feels as it enters and exits your body.

With your eyes still closed, visualize a situation in which you're experiencing change. This could be a change in your personal life, work life, or anything else you'd like to focus on. See it clearly in your mind's eye.

Allow yourself to feel any emotions that come up as you visualize this change. This could be fear, uncertainty, excitement, stress, or any number of other emotions. Notice these feelings without judgment. However you are feeling about this change is okay. It is valid.

With your eyes still closed, repeat the following phrases to yourself: "I embrace change. I am open to new experiences and opportunities. I am being gentle with myself in the midst of these changes."

Now imagine going into the situation you visualized earlier, but you're stepping into it with a sense of peace, a sense of acceptance. See yourself successfully navigating these changes with ease and confidence.

Take a few deep breaths, and when you're ready, open your eyes. Take a moment to reflect on how you feel, and if you'd like to, write these thoughts down in your journal as well.

Gemini Season Affirmations

Here are some affirmations to connect to the energy of Gemini season. If these affirmations do not resonate with you, feel free to adapt them to fit your needs while still channeling the energy of Gemini.

I welcome fresh perspectives.

I am a smart, flexible, and adaptive person.

I embrace change and all of its possibilities.

I am kind to myself in the midst of life's changes.
I am open to developing and changing.
I am able to openly and honestly express myself.
I have access to my imagination and creative side.
I love and accept all the different sides of myself.

Gemini Season Journal Prompts

With the start of the Gemini season, what changes am I most looking forward to?

How can I commit to showing up for myself in the midst of life's changes?

How can I welcome the changes that are coming my way right now?

How can I practice patience in trusting the process of change?

Is there anything I need to change to help support my well-being?

Gemini Season Card Spread

This five-card tarot/oracle spread focuses on the energy of the sun in Gemini. To do a card spread, shuffle the cards and fan them out in front of you, face down. Then pick five cards that you feel most drawn to and use them for reflection with the questions below.

1. What is my primary theme for Gemini season?

2. What aspects of my life might benefit from Gemini energy?

3. What fresh possibilities could materialize during Gemini season?

4. What part of myself might I like to express more?

5. To make room for change in my life, what do I need to let go of?

Crystals for Gemini Season

Blue agate represents focus, balance, and stabilization. It's a grounding presence that helps with clear thinking.

Citrine represents mental clarity, attention, and creativity. It complements a quick wit and the flexibility of energy present during Gemini season.

Aquamarine represents self-expression and can help with clarity of communication.

Sodalite is a stone that fosters spirituality and intuition. It can help with tapping into inner wisdom.

Fluorite increases mental clarity, attention, and organization, and it can aid in concentration.

Herbs for Gemini Season

Lemon balm is for stress relief and can help with relaxation, attention, and mental clarity.

Lemon verbena connects to energy and vitality. It can increase energy levels and elevate mood.

Sage is linked to clarity and intuition; this plant can help with listening and connecting to our inner voice during Gemini season.

Bergamot has a balancing yet invigorating effect on the mind and emotions.

Dill has a calming effect on the mind and can be great for stress relief and relaxation.

GEMINI CORRESPONDENCES

Planet: Mercury. Mercury is the planet of communication. Known as the Messenger, Mercury has information that it wants to share. Mercury is quick-witted, inquisitive, and flexible, and it possesses strong problem-solving and decision-making abilities. Mercury expresses itself through Gemini with its need to communicate and spread information through ways such as writing, teaching, public speaking, and broadcasting.

Color: Yellow. The color yellow is connected to joy, optimism, and positivity. It's a bright hue that symbolizes happiness, friendliness, and cheer. It attracts attention and conveys enthusiasm. It's also related to the sun, warmth, and sunshine. Yellow is also interpreted as a symbol of caution.

Element: Air. The air element represents intelligence, communication, ideas, knowledge, inquisitiveness, quick thinking, and adaptability. Many see the air element as a harmonizer and connector and associate it with the mind. Air signs are known for being articulate, friendly, and great conversationalists. They thrive on learning new things and absorbing information in all forms. Air signs get things moving, which is why they're also known as the "winds of change." They also can be visionaries and forward thinkers. We see the air element expressed through Gemini in their wit, thirst for knowledge, and spreading of information.

Modality: Mutable. In astrology, modalities show us how the signs operate and the role they play in the astrological calendar to help move us through the year. Mutable signs transition us to the next season from the one we're in. Gemini, being a mutable sign, adapts to what's in front of it and leaves behind what is not.

Symbol: The Twins. The Twins represent Gemini's duality. Geminis are renowned for their versatility and adaptability and find it simple to bounce between various pursuits and personalities. The Twins symbol also represents Gemini's ability to see both sides of a situation, and also their ability to be spontaneous and approach life from multiple angles.

House: Third House of Communication. Gemini governs the third house in astrology, which is related to intelligence, information, and communication. It rules the mind and how you perceive the information you receive. It's how you learn, speak, write, edit, think, read, and work with your surroundings. It's also about analyzing and problem-solving.

Polarity Sign: Sagittarius. The Gemini-Sagittarius axis is the axis of knowledge. This polarity is about communication and philosophy, adaptability and adventure, and intellect and expansion. Sagittarius is linked to the desire for exploration and growth, while Gemini is linked to the capacity for thought and communication. Sagittarius relates to expansion, exploration, and philosophy. They are known for having intellectual and spiritual interests and are frequently drawn to professions that provide them the freedom to voice their opinions. Gemini teaches us how to acquire knowledge, while Sagittarius teaches us what to do with it.

Tarot Card: The Lovers. The Lovers card represents choices and decisions we make in life and is linked to the ideas of love, attraction, and connection. The card depicts the time when two individuals first meet and create a relationship. It also represents a joining of forces and energies, indicating kindred spirits and intense bonds. The Lovers is about the importance of creating balance and harmony in our relationships and partnerships.

CANCER

We now move from the versatile, playful, and communicative season of Gemini to the nurturing, resilient, and intuitive season of Cancer. While Gemini is all about morphing and adapting to change, Cancer, the fourth sign of the zodiac, is all about feeling the emotional side of change and learning to be kind to ourselves in every phase of life.

Cancer is our first introduction to water signs. Just as water represents emotions, magic, and mystery, the energy of Cancer has great depth and is very in tune with the subconscious side of life.

Cancer is ruled by the moon, and because of this connection, Cancers are often called "moon children." The moon in astrology represents our inner selves, our emotional landscape—the part of ourselves we keep hidden from the world. Because of this, Cancers are known for being incredibly in tune with their emotions and the emotions of others. Reading people could be considered a superpower of theirs. Their key phrase is "I feel," and just like the moon, their emotions are in a constant state of ebb and flow.

While Cancers have the stereotype of being overly emotional, the truth is, they are just incredibly connected to the full spectrum of the emotional experience. You know how when a wave is coming, they say the best thing to do is to dive straight into it? That's how Cancers approach emotions. They're not afraid to dive right in. This gift of connecting with their emotions on a deep level is one of the reasons why a lot of Cancers tend to be creatives and artists.

This connection to their emotions also makes Cancers very compassionate, which is also why we often see them in fields that require advocating for others, as counselors, and in medicine.

Cancer energy is empathetic, loyal, loving, tenacious, intuitive, persistent, caring, and considerate. Some archetypes connected with Cancer are the Counselor, the Psychic, and the Protector. Their element is water, and their elemental symbol is a river stream, which is cleansing, soothing, and aids in the growth of life around them.

Cancer is a cardinal sign, and in the Northern Hemisphere, it ushers in the season of summer. Cancer season, from around June 22nd to July 22nd, always starts on the solstice. If you were born during Cancer season, then Cancer is your sun sign. This kicking off of summer in the Northern Hemisphere also gives Cancer a fun, nostalgic, and sentimental vibe. When you think of summer, what may come to mind is coming home from college, hanging out with friends, and going on road trips and vacations. There's definitely a nostalgic energy in the air when Cancer season rolls around, and that element of nostalgia is one many Cancers have as well. This is why a lot of Cancers also like to connect—and stay connected—to their roots.

And let's not forget: Cancers can be a lot of fun. They've also got a great sense of humor, which is why a handful of famous comedians happen to be Cancers. Let's say you're throwing a party, and a Cancer attends. You know they're going to have a good time. And if this party is for your birthday, a business milestone, or in honor of something else, they'll be there supporting you and celebrating you with bells on. Part of what comes with them being so deeply connected to their emotions is their ability to tap into the fun, celebratory sides of life. When they party, they party *hard*.

Cancer is a sign that teaches us the importance of cultivating the home of our soul. Most of us associate the word *home* with the house we grew up in or now live in, but really, home is a place we design for ourselves. It's a feeling, a state in which we allow ourselves to unwind, relax, and feel protected and comfortable.

Because Cancer is so closely associated with the idea of home, many think this means that all Cancers are homebodies. There are plenty who are, but really, the home element of Cancer has more to do with creating that protected space where one feels safe.

Cancer's symbol is the Crab. Crabs are known for their strong and protective shell, and this represents Cancer's ability to persist, protect, and hide away when needed.

Cancers are also some of the most tough, persistent, resilient, and tenacious folks around. This is one of the reasons they are connected to the Chariot tarot card; they have a keen ability to persist and keep going even when times are tough. I have a sister who's a Cancer, and she's one of the toughest, most resilient people I know.

Whatever life throws her way, she just picks herself up and keeps on going. She's also kind, compassionate, and a huge advocate for people as well as animals. Cancers really are champions for others, which is something I love about the sign.

However, at times, this can lead to Cancers putting their needs last in favor of the needs of others, which is something they have to watch out for. They are loyal to the bone—the epitome of a ride-or-die. When they're on your side, they'll be there for life. If you have a Cancer in your corner, then you are incredibly lucky.

Cancers are also known for having a strong intuition and a gift for reading other people (which is why one of their archetypes is the Psychic). They tend to have a sixth sense about things and can pick up energies that others might not detect. This also makes them incredibly understanding.

Their ability to understand others is seen in Cancer's house, the fourth house of home and family (chosen or otherwise). This is why one of Cancer's gifts is their ability to provide nurturing spaces for people to feel loved, safe, accepted, and protected. Whether that's on a small or large scale, Cancers have a light about them, and just like the moon, they are able to provide light to others—even in life's darkest moments.

CANCER SEASON THEME

The Crab is the symbol for Cancer and indicates the sign's hard exterior and soft core, as well as its ability to withdraw behind its shell when necessary to protect itself. During this season, then, we focus on protecting our energy. It's one of the most crucial things we can do for our well-being—it's essential because it allows us to prioritize ourselves and keep ourselves balanced. When we protect our energy, we're less likely to become exhausted or experience burnout. We're also better able to cope with challenging situations.

The truth is, we're limited in the amount of energy we can expend. All of us are. And when our energy is depleted, we need to recharge it. We cannot run on no charge. Meanwhile, so many things can affect our energy—our jobs, the media, our romantic relationships, our friendships, our family, and social media. All these things can play significant roles in how we feel. Typically, we start the day with a clean slate of energy, and the things we do during the day impact it either favorably or unfavorably.

There was a time in my life when I wasn't good at protecting my energy. I overworked myself and never took any time to rest. I gave too much of myself to other people. I allowed others to treat me poorly. I allowed the negative energy of others to enter my orbit and my consciousness. I had a really hard time saying no to people. The stress that came from not protecting my energy bled into all areas of my life.

But then I started protecting my energy and respecting my peace, and I watched my life change for the better. I started to note who made me feel good when I was around them and made a point to spend more time with those people. I paid attention to the type of media I was consuming, and I started focusing more on the content I found uplifting. I became comfortable with saying no to things that didn't serve me. I made a point to pay attention to when I needed more rest. Once I started protecting my energy in these ways, I felt a lot less stressed and just happier all around.

The thing about protecting our energy is that what works for one person might not work for the next. Everyone has different energetic limits, and it's about knowing and understanding yours. It comes down to taking inventory of the things in your life and then putting up boundaries as you see fit. Remember, boundaries are a good thing—a healthy thing. And while setting boundaries is not always easy, having them often leads to more peace and contentment.

When it comes to protecting your energy, trust your instincts. Follow your gut. Listening to that intuition is something Cancers are so good at. Listen to that inner voice of yours. And just like the Crab that represents Cancer, remember that you too are allowed to protect yourself and retreat to your "home," to that safe space, whenever you need to.

CANCER SEASON RITUAL

This Cancer season ritual focuses on the water element and connecting to Cancer's planetary ruler, the moon, by making moon water. This is a great exercise in mindfulness and a wonderful way to connect with the watery energy of Cancer season. Creating moon water is best done during a full or new moon, but you can do it whenever you feel inspired.

For this ritual, you need a glass, jar, or ceramic container. You can gather any herbs, dried flowers, or crystals to put them in your moon water, if you like.

Cleanse the container and fill it up with clean water. If you want to put anything besides water in the jar (herbs, dried flowers, crystals), this is the time to add them. Drinking the moon water is an option, but if you decide to do that, make sure that any additives are safe for consumption, and have a lid for your container.

Next, set an intention for the moon water. You can simply set one in your mind, or you can write it on the jar or container. Your intention could be for any desired outcome—healing, abundance, love, confidence. It can also be an affirmation like "I am loved."

Finally, place the container where it will be exposed to moonlight. This could be on a windowsill or outdoor balcony, backyard, or anywhere else outside.

Let the moonlight shine directly on the water for at least an hour. When the time is up, remove the container from the moonlight and store the moon water in a cool place until you're ready to use it.

There are lots of different options for what to do. You can drink it (as long as the ingredients are safe for consumption), add it to your bath, sprinkle it around your home, or use it in any other rituals.

CANCER SEASON MEDITATION

Here's a meditation to protect your energy and connect with Cancer season energy. You can do this meditation seated or lying down, whatever is most comfortable for you.

Start this practice by closing your eyes and taking a few deep breaths in through your nose and out through your mouth. After a few more deep breaths, do an energy check to evaluate how you feel. Are you calm? Grounded? Peaceful? Are you feeling stressed? Burnt out? Tired? After tuning in to how you feel, if there's any lingering tension in your body, take a moment to release it.

Now, with your eyes still closed, imagine a bright light over your head. Let this light create a bubble around you, a protective shield that surrounds you from head to toe.

When this shield is around you, no energy can get in unless you allow it to. It's a boundary that you've set. You are in control. You have the power.

As you continue to visualize this shield around you, think about what kind of energy makes you feel good and what kind of energy you want to be around. What fills your cup? What recharges you? And what does it feel like to have that sort of energy surrounding you? Sit with that feeling.

After taking a few more deep breaths, with your eyes still closed, repeat the following phrases:

I am allowed to protect my energy from the things that don't best serve me.

I am allowed to set boundaries as I see fit.

I am allowed to recharge when my energy is depleted.

I am allowed to fill my cup.

After taking a few more deep breaths, slowly open your eyes. Anytime you need it, imagine that protective shield. Carry it with you. And remember: you are worthy of having peace in your life, and you are in control of what and whom you allow into it.

Cancer Season Affirmations

Here are some affirmations to connect to the energy of Cancer season. If these affirmations don't resonate with you, feel free to adapt them to fit your needs.

I am safe and loved.

I am worthy of care and support.

I am strong and capable of facing any challenge that comes my way.

I am surrounded by people who love and support me.

I am at peace and in harmony with myself and with the world around me.

I am grateful for the gift of life and for all of its possibilities.

I am allowed to protect my energy.

I am in control of what kind of energy I allow into my life.

Cancer Season Journal Prompts

What gives me a sense of security and love?

What self-care activities do I find enjoyable and allow me to unwind?

How do I feel when I'm in the company of kind, encouraging people who match my energy?

Is there anything I need to release or let go of in order to move forward?

What actions can I take to take care of and support my emotional needs?

Cancer Season Card Spread

This five-card tarot/oracle spread focuses on the energy of the sun in Cancer. To do a card spread, shuffle the cards and fan them out in front of you, face down. Then pick five cards that you feel most drawn to and use them for reflection with the questions below.

1. How can I connect with my emotions and intuition during Cancer season?

2. What lessons must I learn to move forward, and how can I overcome any challenges or obstacles that may be in my way?

3. What can I do to nurture and support myself emotionally right now in my life?

4. What old habits or patterns may be holding me back, and how can I let go of them to make space for new growth?

5. How can I find peace and release any negative or unwanted energies that may be affecting my well-being?

Crystals for Cancer Season

Moonstone is connected with lunar energies, intuition, and emotions. It supports your connection to your emotions and intuition and helps you feel more balanced and peaceful.

Pearl has to do with imagination, wisdom, and security. It encourages creativity and is also great for meditating on what makes you feel secure in your life, as well as for connecting to your inner wisdom.

Peridot is linked to transformation and growth, and it can aid you in letting go of things that no longer serve you. It helps you connect with the inner resilience and strength associated with Cancer season.

Selenite cleanses unwanted energies and brings fresh energy into a space. It protects from negative energy as well.

Calcite has calming and soothing properties and can be an energy amplifier—meaning that it can boost energy levels. It can help foster feelings of peace and reduce stress.

Herbs for Cancer Season

Basil has a calming and balancing effect. It can help you feel a sense of inner comfort and evoke feelings of home.

Valerian promotes relaxation and decreases stress. It can help with rest and sleep, increase dream recall, and ease feelings of stress and worry.

Cilantro has protective and purifying properties, and its fresh aroma can clear the air and renew energy. Similarly, it can assist with protecting energy and releasing old energy.

Dandelion promotes healing and feeling grounded and connected to the earth.

Fennel stimulates imagination and creativity. It assists you in embracing your creative side and getting in touch with your intuition.

CANCER CORRESPONDENCES

Planet: Moon. Beautiful and full of mystery, the moon is the planetary ruler of Cancer. It represents our inner selves, emotions, and how we feel and process feelings. It's about the unconscious mind, and it's connected to feminine energy, intuition, imagination, self-care, and exploring the things that help us to heal and grow. And as the moon goes through an eight-phase cycle, it also represents our cycles of life and how we experience the constant ebb and flow of change.

Color: Silver. The color silver is often associated with intuition, mystery, elegance, and healing. With its bright, reflective nature, it's connected to reflection and introspection. Many believe that silver has spiritual and healing properties, and some wear it to promote health, wealth, protection, and peace.

Element: Water. The water element is linked to the unconscious mind, emotions, creativity, imagination, and intuition. It symbolizes our connection to our inner selves as well as to the spiritual world. Water signs are perceptive, inventive, and creative as well as incredibly empathetic and strong readers of energy. And just like water, they nurture and cleanse the world around them and aid in new growth. Water—especially the ocean—also has a degree of mystery, vastness, and wonder to it. It's deep, just like water signs. We see water expressed in Cancers' sensitivity to the world around them as well as in their intuition.

Modality: Cardinal. In astrology, modalities show us how the signs operate and reveal the role they play in the astro-logical calendar to help move us through the year. Cardinal signs always initiate new seasons. Cancers initiate emotional bonds and feelings.

Symbol: The Crab. The crab, known for its robust shell, represents Cancer's ability to persist, protect, and hide away when needed. This is a metaphor for how those born under the sign of Cancer frequently have a thick emotional wall separating them from the outer world. The crab also has a strong capacity to sense its environment by using its numerous sensitive feelers, which is reflected in Cancer's strong intuition and emotional intelligence.

House: Fourth House of Home. The fourth house is the house of home in astrology. As noted earlier, *home* doesn't necessarily mean the place where we live; it represents the metaphorical home we create for ourselves. It's a place where we feel safe, stable, protected, and accepted. The fourth house is a very private and personal place, and it's linked to our deepest emotions and needs. It's also connected to nurturing—how we nurture and how we want to be nurtured.

Polarity Sign: Capricorn. Cancer and Capricorn are the foundation axis in astrology—the axis of home and career. Capricorn is about legacy, and Cancer is about roots. They are both cardinal signs. As a water sign, Cancer represents the emotional foundation of life and, ruled by the moon, it's about nurturing our deepest desires and what we need to feel safe and comforted. It's also linked to compassion and empathy. On the other hand, Capricorn, an earth sign, represents responsibility, discipline, and legacy. Ruled by Saturn, it relates to the lessons we learn to get to where we want to be in life. These energies work together to balance our inner needs and exterior desires. Cancer can teach us lessons on how to feel, while Capricorn can teach us lessons on how to persist—and both signs are known for being incredibly resilient.

Tarot Card: The Chariot. The empowering Chariot represents triumph, achievement, resilience, and tenacity. It stands for the strength to overcome obstacles and move toward your objectives. The card is also a reminder that you are in charge of your life and that you have the persistence and power to bring about anything you want. It also represents making progress and having the fortitude to face any challenges that may come your way.

5

LEO

We now move from the nurturing, resilient, and intuitive season of Cancer to the warm, expressive, and courageous season of Leo. The energy moves us from connecting to our inner selves to how we express ourselves outwardly and bravely allowing ourselves to shine.

This zodiac sign has major main character energy. Think of Leos as human sunshine—bright, sunny, and with the ability to exude light and joy wherever they go. It makes sense, as their planetary ruler is the sun.

The sun is very much at home in Leo. It loves to be there. Because of this, the energy of the sun radiates strongest through this sign, beaming and shining freely. The sun is a star, the center of our solar system. All the planets revolve around it. It's the same with Leo. Just as it's hard to turn away from the sun, it's hard to look away from Leo energy.

The sun is also a giver of life and a mood booster. It provides us with warmth and feeds us with nutrients. Life on Earth could not survive without the light of the sun. While Cancer, the sign that precedes Leo, is ruled by the moon and *reflects* the light of the sun, Leo *emits* it. Leo energy is not only about shining bright themselves, but also about being a light for others.

Leo is the fifth sign in the astrological calendar. In the Northern Hemisphere, Leo takes place during the summer, and it's a fixed sign, meaning it personifies the essence of the season. Being a fixed sign gives Leos a headstrong quality. When they are passionate about something, they are stubborn and stay steadfast in their beliefs. Their element is fire, and their elemental symbol is a bonfire that everyone gathers around for warmth and comfort.

The sun is in Leo from around July 23rd to August 22nd, and if you were born during Leo season, your sun sign is Leo. The energy of this sign is creative, brave, loyal, generous, encouraging, warm, and entertaining. Its key phrase is "I lead," and Leos have a knack for leading the way, even when they're not trying to. They are great at stepping up and taking charge when called, partly because they don't mind being in the spotlight and partly because they're confident in their skills.

This leadership quality is also symbolized in their element, fire. Fire can illuminate a dark path and can be a guide. Leos, then, are talented at guiding people and encouraging them along in their journey.

Leos are renowned for their creative abilities and ingenuity. They also place importance on their presentation. This can manifest in how they dress, how they decorate their home, and how they bring their creativity into the world.

They have a natural magnetism and charisma that draws others to them. This is why lots of Leos (and people with strong Leo placements in their birth charts) are often entertainers, politicians, and other positions where they are—or will become—well-known and have influence.

Just to be clear, not all Leos may resonate with the archetype of the Performer or the Entertainer, but they all have the power to shine if they choose to.

Their performative quality stems from their ability to have fun and to play. They are good at keeping their authentic selves alive. Leo energy, then, can help teach us to foster love for our true selves, allowing them to come out and play.

And wherever a Leo goes, attention often follows. Leos have a keen ability to attract attention—and direct it. This means that if you want to feel good, find yourself a Leo who loves you. They like to dote on people they care about. Leos are the friends who bring a smile to your face, who add warmth to your life, who help and encourage you. Despite what some may think, Leos have no problem sharing the stage with those they love. Leos are also incredibly loyal and dedicated to those near and dear to them.

I have an auntie who is a Leo, and she has this beautiful energy that everyone seems to gather around like a moth to a flame. Her home is cozy and inviting, and whenever anyone's around her, they just feel good! She remembers details and little things about everyone that makes them feel special. She's so much fun, and someone people just want to be around.

That's something I love about Leos; just like the fire that we all gather around, they can offer comfort, even when we don't even realize we need it.

Leo's symbol is the Lion, which is why this sign is also associated with royalty. Leos are definitely the rulers of their own kingdoms. This kingdom may be their home, a creation of theirs, their dream job, or something else.

Regardless of what it is, every Leo is the ruler of their own castle, their own fortress.

Their symbol, the Lion, indicates the strength inherent in the sign. Leos are also known for being brave and courageous, for not backing away from a challenge, and for being determined and going after the things they want in life. Often when Leos seek to achieve something, they do. They have the eye of the tiger. And they strive to be the best—mainly, their best selves. When they do something, they do it to the fullest. They go after it with every fiber of their being.

One of the most admirable things about the sign is its generosity and kindness. Leos are incredibly giving—of their time, love, attention, affection, and affirmation. They'll give you the shirt off their back if you need it, or gifts. Being generous makes them feel good. They may be the sign of the roaring lion, but inside, they are big softies.

The bottom line is, at their core, Leos just want to spread their light. That could look like performing for you, giving you gifts or throwing you a party, encouraging you, creating for you, or having you over to hang out.

Regardless of how a Leo chooses to spread their light, one thing's for certain: they do it brightly.

LEO SEASON THEME

For this season's well-being theme, we draw inspiration from Leo's planetary ruler, the sun, and focus on shining through self-expression.

The sun is the center of the universe, and this reminds us that we're at the center of our lives, the main character in our stories. It reminds us to be loud and proud of who we are, to celebrate ourselves, and to express ourselves freely.

Self-expression is the way we communicate our ideas and emotions and share our opinions and life experiences with the world. It's a crucial part of human growth and can have a big effect on our overall well-being. Expression includes verbal communication, writing, art, music, dancing, fashion, and many other kinds of creativity.

Self-expression may sound easy enough, but it's often too easy to neglect. This is not by any fault of our own. It's easy to fall under the influence of the messages that people throughout our lives, as well as society, tell us about how we should be. These messages can repress our self-expression.

Expressing yourself authentically is the goal here. It's about expressing the version of yourself that makes you happy, the one that doesn't give a damn what anybody thinks. Your authentic version doesn't try to live up to other people's standards or expectations; it's creative and free.

Do you ever think how you would express yourself if you truly didn't care what anyone thought of you? What would you do with your life? How different would you act in your daily life? Consider how many people out there are living life a bit repressed, and not expressing themselves freely out of worry of what others might think, or fear for how they might be treated.

Have you ever noticed how many children are authentically themselves? They express themselves freely and don't care what anybody else thinks of them. But once we reach a certain age, that magic starts to fizzle, in large part because of our fear of being judged (of course, things like trauma can be factors too). So many of us lose that childlike wonder, that ability to be who we authentically *are*.

As a child, I expressed myself by way of singing, performing, dancing, writing plays for me and my siblings and friends to act in, and then directing the plays that we performed in front of all our parents. When someone came over to my house, I made them perform, play dress-up, run around in the backyard with toy swords— pretending we were warriors—or swim in the pool, pretending we were mermaids. It was always something fun and imaginative. I kept singing in plays and performing in shows, and I really enjoyed it. As a kid, I didn't care what anybody thought about it.

But then I reached junior high and started to care about what my peers thought of me, and I carried that into my adult years. I reached a point in my late 20s when I realized I was repressing those sides of myself, and I started shedding my skin and reconnecting with the parts I had kept hidden for so long. I'm happy that I allowed those parts to come out and play again.

Relearning self-expression doesn't always come easily. For some, it can be challenging and require openness, kindness, and patience. Additionally, self-expression can look different depending on the person. Some people express more subtly than others. There are many ways to approach it, and no way is right or wrong. The key is just to be in touch with our true selves and the things that make us happiest.

When the sun is in Leo, it's prime time to foster self-expression and to connect with those parts of ourselves that bring us joy. It's time to let that part of you come forward and shine. Let it play, let it be the star of the show, let it be free.

Regardless of what self-expression looks like for you—writing, playing music, dressing up and going out, cooking, sports, painting, or styling outfits—you'll find even more love for yourself in the process. And just as Leo beams like the sun, I hope you allow yourself to shine bright and radiate like the light that you truly are.

LEO SEASON RITUAL

This Leo season ritual focuses on tapping into your creativity. This practice is meant to help you explore your creative side and express yourself.

To begin, find a place where you feel relaxed and inspired to do something creative. This could be a room in your house, outside at a park, or even a corner of a coffee shop—wherever you feel most comfortable.

Next, gather whatever materials you need for a creative endeavor. This could look like sheet music and an instrument, paints, a notebook and pen, a camera or tablet, and so on.

Before you begin, take a few deep breaths in through your nose and out through your mouth, and release any tension in your body. When you're ready, set an intention for your creative ritual. The intention could be to have fun, to relieve stress, or to express an emotion.

Next, it's time to create! Turn off nearby devices and let your imagination run free. Don't worry about the outcome. Instead, focus on being mindful and enjoying the process. If you find yourself getting stuck, take a break and come back with a fresh perspective. The idea is to enjoy yourself, not to make it stressful.

Once you've finished, take a moment to reflect on what you've created. What emotions come up? How does it make you feel?

When you're done, take a few deep breaths and be proud of yourself for doing something creative that helps you express yourself and brings you joy. You can return to this practice whenever you feel inspired to do so.

LEO SEASON MEDITATION

Here's a self-love meditation to connect with Leo season energy:

To begin, find a comfortable place where you can sit or lie down. Take a few slow, deep breaths in through your nose and out through your mouth, and release any lingering tension in your body. Start with your feet and move up through your legs, your torso and arms, and then your neck, face, and head.

Now, focus your attention on the breath entering your body and then flowing out from it. Feel your stomach expand on every inhale and contract on every exhale.

As you continue to breathe deeply, imagine a warm, golden light surrounding your body, enveloping you in a cocoon of comfort.

Now repeat the following affirmations to yourself, silently or out loud: "I am worthy of love," "I am enough," "I am loved," "I am kind to myself," and "I accept myself where I am right now."

Sit with these feelings of self-love and self-acceptance for a few deep breaths. If any negative thoughts arise, acknowledge them, then return your focus to the affirmations and your breath.

When you're ready, slowly open your eyes and take a few more deep breaths. Take a moment to reflect on how you feel, and carry self-love with you as you return to the motions of your day.

Leo Season Affirmations

I am filled with warmth, joy, and abundance.
I am strong, courageous, and determined.
I am creative, imaginative, and inspired.
I am open to new beginnings and new opportunities.
I am connected to my own inner wisdom and guidance.
I am worthy and deserving of happiness and abundance.
I am confident and self-assured.
I am full of energy, vitality, and enthusiasm.

Leo Season Journal Prompts

What are the qualities and characteristics of Leo that resonate with me? How can I tap into these qualities during this season?

What is my inner fire and passion, and how can I connect with and nurture these qualities?

What are some ways I can express myself during Leo season? How can I use the energy of Leo season to motivate me with this intention?

How can I connect with my own inner wisdom and guidance during this time? What messages and insights await me?

Leo Season Card Spread

This five-card tarot/oracle spread focuses on the energy of the sun in Leo. To do a card spread, shuffle the cards and fan them out in front of you, face down. Then pick five cards that you feel most drawn to and use them for reflection with the questions below.

1. What is the theme of Leo season for me?

2. What inner strength and determination do I need to tap into?

3. How can I tap into my creativity and imagination?

4. In what ways can I nurture more of my self-expression?

5. What new opportunities and possibilities should I be open to during this season?

Crystals for Leo Season

Sunstone bears the name of the sun, the planet that rules Leo. It's a crystal of vigor, inventiveness, and excitement. It may also help increase passion and a sense of adventure.

Ruby represents passion, energy, and vitality. It helps you become more courageous, strong, and self-assured.

Amber represents power, vitality, and creativity. It can help you connect to your imagination.

Tiger's eye represents confidence, courage, and determination. It can help with motivation to reach your goals and with staying focused.

Gold calcite represents charm and radiance and is considered an energy amplifier. It enhances natural charisma and helps you shine even brighter.

Herbs for Leo Season

Marjoram represents love, compassion, kindness, and healthy relationships and is linked to the fire element. Due to its symbolic connections to the qualities of Leo, it can help assist in fostering feelings of love and compassion.

Marigold promotes confidence, courage, and joy. It can assist with connecting to inner strength, confidence, and leadership abilities, as well as with attracting success.

Thyme promotes fortitude, bravery, and tenacity, and it can increase resilience. Many use it to assist with overcoming obstacles and embracing the bravery of Leo energy.

Calendula promotes vigor, inventiveness, and confidence. It can help you feel more energized, passionate, and confident.

Bay laurel brings good fortune and protects against negative energies.

LEO CORRESPONDENCES

Planet: Sun. The sun is a star and one of the most significant celestial bodies in astrology. It's the focal point of the solar system and the origin of all life on Earth. It represents identity, self, purpose, vitality, power, and main character energy. It is how one shines.

Color: Gold. When you think of gold, you might think of riches, success, luxury, and beauty. Gold is a sign of wealth and power in many cultures, and they frequently link it to the sun, a potent symbol of rebirth, vitality, and energy. Because gold is a strong, long-lasting metal that doesn't tarnish or corrode, it also brings forth the idea of eternity. It also represents confidence and abundance.

Element: Fire. Enthusiasm, passion, warmth, zeal, inspiration, and leadership are all correlated with the fire element. Aries, Leo, and Sagittarius are fire signs in the zodiac and are characterized by their confidence, bravery, and independence. Fire signs relate to vigor, passion, and creativity.

They can be motivated by their aspirations and goals and possess a strong spirit of exploration and adventure. Fire signs have a strong sense of identity and an independent spirit. They are risk-takers and experimental by nature, and they bring their lively, dynamic energy to any situation. Fire is a symbol of renewal and purification because it can burn away the old and make room for the new. It brings light and warmth, which can be both comforting and inspiring. Fire can help light one's own path and also fuel others. We see the fire element expressed through Leo in their warmth and ability to shine.

Modality: Fixed. In astrology, modalities show us how the signs operate and the role they play in the astrological calendar to help move us through the year. Fixed signs help stabilize the season and are the pillar and essence of the season they are in. Leo, as a fixed sign, shines their light on the world around them.

Symbol: The Lion. The Lion is a symbol of courage, strength, and royalty, as the Lion is the king of the animals. It connects to the attributes of leadership, confidence, bravery, nobility, generosity, and compassion. The Lion symbolizes some of the properties of the sun: vigor, energy, and warmth. It's also a strong and motivating symbol that reflects a person's capacity to lead and make their presence known in the world.

House: Fifth House of Self-Expression. The fifth house in astrology is connected to romance, self-expression, joy, and creativity and is ruled by Leo. We frequently associate it with a person's capacity for artistic, musical, literary, fashion, or other kind of self-expression. Playfulness, as well as a person's hobbies and leisure pursuits, are also connected to the fifth house. It's also about the pleasure of being alive and focusing on the things that foster happiness and joy.

Polarity Sign: Aquarius. Leo and Aquarius are the axis of expression. Leo is about self-expression, and Aquarius is about group expression. They are both fixed signs. Leo, a fire sign, is linked to imagination, individuality, and leadership. Aquarius, an air sign, is linked to creativity, uniqueness, and altruism. It also relates to the yearning for independence and intellectual curiosity. Together, the energies of Leo and Aquarius stand for a harmony between warmth and originality, self-expression, and freedom. In addition, both Leo and Aquarius have a strong desire to stand out and be different, and also to be caring and generous. Leo can teach us lessons on how to love and accept ourselves, while Aquarius can teach us lessons on how to love and accept the collective.

Tarot Card: Strength. The Strength card relates to internal fortitude, bravery, and tenacity. It can represent someone's capacity to overcome difficulties with their own inner power and strength. The card often has an image of a woman and a lion on it, which symbolizes a person's ability to face fear and uncertainty with courage. The card is also about connecting to our inner strength and power and reminds us that we're strong enough to make it through any obstacle that comes our way.

6

VIRGO

We now move from the warm, expressive, and courageous season of Leo to the refined, skillful, and healing season of Virgo. While Leo season is all about being bold and creative, the energy shift in Virgo season is more about enduring and cleansing. It's slower and more methodical, as good things take time. Leo teaches us how to shine and bravely express who we want to be, and Virgo shows us how to become more skillful in the things we are passionate about.

There's a saying that goes, "If you want something done right, ask a Virgo." Okay, that's not quite it—it's actually, "If you want something done right, do it yourself." I like my version, though, because it holds a lot of truth. No one quite does something "right" like a Virgo does. They just have a knack for doing things really well.

Virgos are the sixth sign of the zodiac and are renowned for their practicality, meticulousness, and work ethic. They're excellent at getting things done efficiently.

Additionally, they're known for their analytical thinking and problem-solving skills. Let's just say that if you have a problem you can't quite find a solution for, call your Virgo friend. And if you're looking for an opinion about a book or a film or a new restaurant to try, ask that friend too, because they probably have a really good one.

Virgos are the fixers, the organizers—the ones that make things happen. They solve problems and find solutions. A gift of theirs is being able to make order out of even the most chaotic of situations. They notice things that shouldn't be there. They're almost like a microscope at times, able to see the cracks and inconsistencies that others might miss. They have an amazing attention to detail.

The sun is in Virgo from around August 23rd to September 22nd, and if you were born during Virgo season, then Virgo is your sun sign. They are a mutable sign, meaning they transition us into a new season, helping the cosmic tides to turn. In the Northern Hemisphere, they transition us from summer to fall. It's almost a back-to-school vibe that goes along with Virgo—the idea that summer vacation is over and it's time to get organized.

Virgo is ruled by the planet Mercury, but how Mercury expresses itself in Virgo is a little different from how it expresses itself in Gemini. In Gemini, Mercury is a lot more communicative and likes to spread information. When in Virgo, it's more about analytical and critical thinking, making people more detail oriented in their speech and thought. Being a Mercury-ruled sign also makes Virgos seekers of knowledge and clarity, and they tend to enjoy acquiring new information.

They strive for self-improvement, and as such are talented at taking the information they learn and applying it to their lives. This is why wisdom is also a trait that goes along with the sign and one that's echoed in their corresponding tarot card, the Hermit.

The Hermit card as it corresponds to Virgo is also about shedding light on things and using one's analytical mind to make wise decisions. It ties into their key phrase: "I analyze." This speaks to Virgos' knack for attention to all the details and thoroughly thinking things through. They are not ones to just act impulsively—they move with intention.

Learning how to hone a skill is a talent that comes naturally to Virgos. They have a strong level of dedication to whatever they set their sights on—and they often do a really good job.

Do you know the phrase "practice makes perfect"? When you repeat a skill enough, you improve. I like to think that "practice makes perfect" is the unofficial motto for Virgo. They're constantly refining and improving, and they feel invigorated when they're developing a skill that brings them satisfaction and happiness. Virgos are the people who try different recipes until they get them just right; who show up for basketball practice a few hours early, just to get a few more shots in; who proofread that paper again and again just to make sure they didn't miss any typos; who practice a dance routine until it looks exactly how they want it to. They often strive for greatness in all that they do. They can lean toward perfectionism and are often hard on themselves—they're their own worst critics, which is something they need to keep an eye on.

Virgo energy is analytical, dedicated, practical, hardworking, healing, trustworthy, and helpful. The symbols for Virgo are the Maiden, the Virgin, and the one that I like to use: the Goddess—more specifically, the goddess of the harvest, a woman who holds wheat to nourish and feed those around her.

Virgo rules the sixth house of health, which makes its energy also very grounding, healing, and service-oriented. Virgos like to help out whenever they can.

They are an earth sign, and their elemental symbol is trees in a forest. While they are rooted into the ground, trees can still change, depending on the season (that is, their leaves transform in the fall, and they lose their leaves going into winter). This symbolism also speaks to Virgos being a mutable earth sign, which makes them a little more flexible than other earth signs—though their flexibility still comes with practicality. They are not as random and spontaneous as the other mutable signs, as Virgos carry the dedication and dependability that comes with being an earth sign.

Take Beyoncé. If you've ever seen any behind-the-scenes footage of her getting ready for a tour, you can really glimpse her Virgo energy. She doesn't stop until things are exactly where she wants them to be—she doesn't miss any details. She strives for a certain level of greatness. Her hard work is evident in her choreography, her vocals, her stage presence, her outfits—it's all flaw-less. And yet she has humility and an energy that is very nurturing, helpful, kind, comforting, and encouraging to those around her.

That's something else that Virgos are known for—their humility. It's perhaps because in their minds, nothing they do is ever perfect enough, or because they're good at seeing things for what they are. Regardless of why, they have the ability to be grounded while accomplishing great things. They don't seek out affirmation from others, because impressing themselves is a challenge in itself. I guarantee you this: behind the scenes in education, medicine, law, and politics, there's probably a Virgo quietly and meticulously working hard to get things done without needing any recognition for it.

While no one else has quite the attention to detail and precision in their work and can create well-crafted, polished pieces the way a Virgo does, they inspire us by staying humble and connected to the world around them while also helping others in need.

VIRGO SEASON THEME

For the well-being theme during Virgo season, we pull inspiration from Virgos' natural knack for refining things. Since cleansing, clearing, and rearranging often soothes them, the theme to focus on during Virgo season is clearing—specifically, clearing out clutter, which can refer to physical as well as emotional and energetic clutter. Since Virgo is a mutable sign that helps transition us into a new season in nature, this is a great time to leave behind the old and welcome in the new.

When we think of clutter, we think of things like a drawer stuffed with documents, a messy closet, or a never-ending e-mail inbox. And yes, those things qualify as clutter, but it can be anything you could be holding on to that you don't need in your life.

Unhealthy relationships, overcommitting to activities you don't enjoy, unkind thoughts about yourself, and so on all count as forms of mental and energetic clutter. We can improve our own sense of well-being by making a conscious effort to eliminate the clutter that accumulates in our lives.

Clutter can make you feel like things are out of order and chaotic, which can add to feelings of stress and anxiety. By clearing these things, we can give our spaces a sense of order and peace, which can help us feel more calm.

From an energetic point of view, clutter can also stop the flow of energy in a space, making it feel stuck. Getting rid of the clutter can release the stuck energy, letting a more positive and healthy flow of energy in. Our spaces are energetic extensions of ourselves. The energy in our surroundings affects us—whether we realize it or not.

Getting rid of clutter can help us let go of unwanted energies that may be tied to certain things we have. This can help us move on and feel like we're starting fresh. Decluttering our spaces and minds and releasing things that don't contribute to our growth can make room for things that foster joy. The result is a more tranquil state of mind and increased clarity.

Blockages in our energy field might be the result of holding on to bad thoughts, emotions, and experiences. Things like meditation, rituals, writing, therapy, energy healing, yoga, or any practice that resonates with you can help you cleanse mental and energetic clutter.

And for the physical clutter, you can start small. Declutter a few things at a time if you don't want to do it all at once, and just work on clearing things out little by little at a pace that works for you.

When it comes to clearing and decluttering, you have a lot of options; feel free to explore and try different things until you find a method that works for you.

Clearing and decluttering things from your life might feel difficult at times, but focusing on it can be very cleansing and can have a significant impact on your health and happiness for the long haul.

VIRGO SEASON RITUAL

The Virgo season ritual focuses on clearing the energy around you with sound. You'll need a singing bowl, chime, bell, or other instrument. If you don't have one of these, you can find a sound online (try YouTube), or search for a specific sound on a music app. If it's available to you, open a window to let some fresh, cleansing air into your space. You can also light some incense or candles if you choose.

Once you're ready, find a comfortable place to sit or lie down. Start by taking a few deep breaths in through your nose and out through your mouth.

Next, set an intention for the space. This could be something like, "I want to cleanse and reset the energy in my space."

Now close your eyes and picture a bright, white light surrounding your body. This represents a cleansing light that purifies the energy in your space. Imagine it getting bigger and bigger until it fills the whole room, pushing out any negative energy along the way.

Now open your eyes and let the singing bowls, chimes, or other sound play in your space. While imagining the white light pushing the negative energy out of your space, also imagine the sound clearing and resetting its energy.

Next, repeat the following affirmations: "This space is full of love, light, and good energy," and "I release any negative energy and welcome in the good."

Take a few more deep breaths and close the ritual by expressing gratitude for the cleansing that has taken place.

VIRGO SEASON MEDITATION

Here's a clearing meditation to connect with Virgo season energy:

Begin by relaxing your body, releasing any tension in your shoulders, jaw, neck, and back. Continue relaxing your body all the way down to your toes.

Now close your eyes and bring your attention to your breath. You don't need to change your breath in any way; just notice it. Pay attention to what it feels like as it flows in and out of your body.

Continue to keep your body relaxed and your awareness on your breath. Be grounded and present in the moment.

If any thoughts arise, notice them without any judgment, and let them flow right through you in the same way that your breath is flowing in and out of your body.

When you do this, you're anchoring your awareness to your breath, pushing away any mental clutter, and allowing yourself to simply *be*.

Continue the process of focusing on your breath for as long as you'd like.

When you're ready, open your eyes. Take a moment to notice the stillness and the relaxation in your body, and carry that feeling of relaxation with you throughout the rest of your day.

Virgo Season Affirmations

Here are some affirmations to connect to the energy of Virgo season. If these affirmations don't resonate with you, feel free to adapt them to fit your needs while still channeling the healing energy of Virgo.

I am organized, detail oriented, and focused on self-improvement.

I am practical, efficient, and capable of achieving my goals.

I am open to new experiences and opportunities for growth.

I am worthy of love, success, and happiness.

I trust in my abilities and am confident in my decisions.

I am grateful for the abundance in my life and am open to receiving more.

I am strong, resilient, and capable of overcoming any challenge.

I am worthy of respect and treat myself and others with kindness and compassion.

Virgo Season Journal Prompts

What are some intentions I'd like to set for myself during Virgo season?

How do I plan to work toward achieving my intentions?

How do I plan to celebrate my progress during this season?

What are some things I'm grateful for in my life, and how can I express gratitude during Virgo season?

Virgo Season Card Spread

This five-card tarot/oracle spread focuses on the energy of the sun in Virgo. To do a card spread, shuffle the cards and fan them out in front of you, face down. Then pick five cards that you feel most drawn to and use them for reflection with the questions below.

1. What's an important lesson to learn during Virgo season?

2. How can I best take care of my health and well-being during Virgo season?

3. How can I hone my daily routine—or change it—during Virgo season?

4. How can I connect with my spiritual side during Virgo season?

5. What opportunities and possibilities are available to me during this Virgo season, and how can I make the most of them?

Crystals for Virgo Season

Amazonite represents self-discovery, communication, and awareness. It can support your quest for self-knowledge and help with communication.

Moss agate represents rebirth and growth. It helps in releasing what no longer serves you to make room for new growth and change.

Sapphire represents wisdom, mental clarity, and inner peace. It's beneficial for seeking spiritual growth and self-improvement.

Smoky quartz is key for anchoring, grounding, and stability. It helps in shielding yourself from negative energies and staying grounded.

Labradorite is about connecting to intuition and stimulating the mind. It helps you connect to your inner voice and gain deeper self-understanding.

Herbs for Virgo Season

Alfalfa attracts prosperity and abundance, and many use it in manifestation rituals. It can assist you in staying focused and reaching your goals.

Milk thistle promotes health and improves overall well-being. It assists in prioritizing self-care and acts as a reminder to put your health first.

Gentian represents willpower and tenacity. It's beneficial for maintaining resolve and focus.

Hops is related to sleep. It helps with relaxation and promotes a feeling of calm.

Parsley represents cleansing and purification. It's beneficial for cleansing and renewing your energy.

VIRGO CORRESPONDENCES

Planet: Mercury. Mercury is the planet of communication. Known as the Messenger, Mercury has information it wants to share. Mercury is quick-witted, inquisitive, flexible, and possesses strong problem-solving and decision-making abilities. Mercury expresses itself through Virgos by being analytical, thinking critically, and being efficient in communication.

Color: Brown. Brown is associated with nature, stability, and consistency. It serves as a metaphor for organic and natural elements because of its associations with things like wood, stone, and soil. It's a neutral color that represents things like sensibility, practicality, and honesty. It often helps promote feelings of warmth, calm, and groundedness.

Element: Earth. The earth element represents stability, growth, practicality, abundance, dependability, safety, and rootedness. It symbolizes the foundation upon which all other things are built and is the essence of the physical and material realm. Earth signs are the builders of the zodiac. They are more "down to earth" and connected to the world around them. They enjoy plans, routine, and security. And just like the earth, they are strong and prosperous. We see the earth element expressed through Virgo in their practicality, healing nature, and dependability.

Modality: Mutable. In astrology, modalities show us how the signs operate and the role they play in the astrological calendar to help move us through the year. Mutable signs transition us to the next season. Virgos, being under a mutable sign, are great at moving from one skill to the next and perfecting whatever they do.

Symbol: The Goddess. There are a few different symbols for Virgo in astrology: the Virgin, the Maiden, and the Goddess. I feel the Goddess most represents Virgo, because she's a symbol of patience, dedication, and practicality, and also because of her focus on nourishing others. Being an earth sign, Virgo is connected to agriculture, and is known as the goddess of the harvest. The Goddess has a strong bond with the soil, and as such is in charge of guaranteeing the crops' fertility. She frequently holds a sheaf of wheat to represent the abundance of the harvest that not only nourishes her, but also others. This speaks to Virgos' desire to help others, as well as their patience and diligence in producing plenty from their hard work.

House: Sixth House of Health. The sixth house in astrology is the house of well-being, daily routines, healing, and vitality. It's ruled by Virgo and is about discipline and organization in our daily routine, as well as taking care of our body and mind. Healing is a big theme of the sixth house!

In addition, this house is about work, service to others, and finding meaning and fulfillment in career.

Polarity Sign: Pisces. Virgo and Pisces are the axis of healing. Virgo is about reminding us to take care of our physical and mental bodies, while Pisces is about caring for our spiritual health. They are both mutable signs. As an earth sign, Virgo is known for its practicality, patience, and skillfulness. Pisces, a water sign, is known for creativity, spirituality, and empathy. It also relates to the subconscious mind and imagination. Virgo is the plan, and Pisces is the dream. Virgo is about the small picture, and Pisces is about the big picture. These energies can work together to shift the focus to healing our mind, body, and spirit. Virgo can teach us the importance of anchoring ourselves and keeping our feet on the ground, while Pisces can teach us the importance of connecting to our higher selves.

Tarot Card: The Hermit. The Hermit card is connected to Virgo as well as the planet Mercury. This card is about wisdom gained in seclusion, meditation, and contemplation: going inward to get some insight. It's about introspection and self-discovery—taking time for reflection and personal growth, to fill your cup and find some peace. It's also about seeking knowledge and gaining wisdom.

7

LIBRA

We now move from the refining, skillful, and healing season of Virgo to the balanced, charming, and relational season of Libra. While self-care during Virgo season was about clearing and removing things from our lives, Libra season builds on that, focusing on cultivating balance and peace in our lives as well as fostering healthy relationships.

Libra is the seventh sign of the zodiac, and this is where we see things start to shift energetically. Libra is the first time we see a polarity in the calendar (it's Aries's polarity sign). The first six signs put the focus on the individual, while the last six shift to focus on the world around us.

When we started the astrological calendar with Aries, the well-being theme was of the self and putting ourselves first. But now, when we get to Libra, it's an opportunity to look at our relationships and connections and how they best serve us, how we show up for others in our relationships, and how we can seek balance in all things.

Libra is a cardinal sign, which means it ushers in a new season in nature. In the Northern Hemisphere, Libra season lines up with the fall equinox. It only makes sense that Libra would initiate autumn, since it's one of the most stunning times of year, and Libra is a sign connected to beauty.

With the colors, the coziness, the fall-themed lattes, the scarves and sweaters . . . there's a charm in the air during autumn that reflects the energy that Libras exude.

Whenever I think of Libra, the first word that comes to my mind is *charm*. Because the thing about Libras is, even if they don't come across as alluring at first, they all have the natural ability to charm you, to have fun with you, to win you over and woo you. And they can make you feel welcome and accepted. There's no sign naturally as charming, able to navigate social situations, and great at maintaining one-on-one partnerships like Libra.

The essence of this sign is rooted in seeking harmony and balance in life. Libra is ruled by the planet Venus just as Taurus is. Venus is all about love, beauty, pleasure, and relationships. While the influence that Venus has on Taurus is more about the pleasure-seeking and abundance aspects, Venus with Libra puts a lot of attention on peace, beauty, and love—which is why Libras are known for being friendly, diplomatic, and happy to be in relationships. They act as great mediators by listening to both sides of a story and try to make sure everyone is treated fairly.

Libra is all about finding balance and harmony in every part of our lives and appreciating the beauty as well. They can find beauty everywhere and in everything and are known for having a good eye for aesthetics and art. This is why many Libras play in the fields of art, design, fashion, and entertainment. And because of their desire for balance and justice, we also see a lot of Libras in politics, law, social work, and other helping professions.

The sun is in Libra from around September 23rd to October 22nd, and if you were born during Libra season, then Libra is your sun sign. Their key phrase is "I balance." The sign's symbol, the Scales, is also about balance—not tipping too far in one direction or the other. It can stand for seeking balance within and around the self—emotional balance, a work-life balance, and so on. Another reason for what's behind the symbol is that the sun goes through the Libra constellation during the equinox, a time linked to equilibrium in nature.

In addition, we see the same desire in Libra's corresponding tarot card: Justice. This card is not only about seeking balance in our lives, but also the balance of justice and fairness in the lives of others and in our community.

Some archetypes connected with the sign are the Peacemaker, the Socialite, the Mediator, and the Creator. Libra energy is fun, charming, harmonious, diplomatic, clever, and social. They are an air sign, and their elemental symbol is a breeze. Think of them as cool and comforting, giving you that sweet embrace you might need on a hot day.

Libras rule the seventh house of relationships and partnerships. Since partnerships are a huge theme for Libra, they can tend to be people pleasers if they're not careful, which is where the stereotype of them being indecisive comes from. The truth is, they just want to make everyone happy. They are friendly and focused on harmony, and they can feel uncomfortable when those around them aren't having a good time. If you ask a Libra where they want to meet for dinner and they say it's up to you, they mean it. They'd rather have you decide and go somewhere you enjoy—they're easygoing in that regard.

I've spent a lot of time around Libras within both my family and friends. One of the biggest things I've observed about their energy is, that they want everyone around them to be at ease. They're great at making people feel comfortable and are great hosts. They're very fair-minded and overall talented at connecting with people.

My youngest brother is a Libra, and something I love about him is how inclusive he is. He has such a wide range of friends, and he's always having them over and hosting them. He makes sure that everyone feels comfortable and no one feels left out. He stands up for his friends. He's fair-minded, incredibly funny and charming, and always has such a balanced outlook on life—even for his very young age. He's good at finding contentment in whatever he's doing—one of the many things I love about him.

I also have a Libra friend who works in local politics. Something I admire about Libras is how they listen to the needs of others and are passionate about fighting for equality. They are personable and genuinely want to improve lives.

Regardless of whether Libras are hosting a fun party, making you feel accepted and comfortable, or fighting for injustices they see in their community, they constantly strive for harmony with others, and I think that's a beautiful thing.

LIBRA SEASON THEME

For our well-being theme during Libra season, we draw inspiration from their key phrase, "I balance," and their ruling house, the seventh house of partnerships. This is about finding balance in our relationships.

Relationships and our connections to others are part of supporting our well-being. This doesn't mean you need to have a lot of friends, constantly connect with people, or be in a romantic relationship. It just means that relationships contribute to our overall happiness, and that maintaining healthy relationships is an important part of taking care of ourselves.

When the sun is in Libra, it's a great time to look at our relationships. We can strive for balance and be kind and loving, making sure we're giving to our relationships as well as receiving from them. And if you so desire, this is the ideal time to prioritize fostering new relationships.

We're social beings by nature—consider our origins, living in tribes and small communities—so everyone (yes, even if you're an introvert) needs to connect in some way with other people. We've evolved to depend on each other, and we flourish when our social connections are strong.

Everyone can approach this need for connection in a different way. It can look like meeting up with friends, joining an online group, or volunteering in your community. Whether it's face-to-face, virtual, or a little bit of each, we all need connection for our mental and physical health.

Isn't it wild to think that a lack of social connection can affect our health? Again, this doesn't mean you need a bunch of people in your life. You just need to connect with one or more people whom you feel comfortable with to nourish that side of your well-being. During this season, you can tap into Libra energy and shift some attention to your connections.

And, since Libra season is also about balance, when you look at your relationships, think about what's working and what might not be. What relationships are nourishing you? Are any draining you?

There was a time in my life, years ago, when I had some relationships that didn't make me feel good and weren't healthy for me, so I made the decision to move away from them. And when I did, I felt such a strong sense of peace—which was confirmation that they weren't good for my well-being. Making a decision to move away from a relationship that doesn't serve you isn't always easy. Of course, circumstances are different in every relationship; there are many facets and layers and complexities. But remember that you *deserve* to be treated well in your relationships. You are worthy of that, and it's more than okay to set boundaries or walk away if you need to.

This season, when you take a look at your relationships, go deep. Ask questions like these: Where do you get your connection from? Who are some people in your life that bring you happiness and joy? How do you show kindness to people? Do you have any relationships that don't serve you well? Do you struggle with loneliness?

And if you're feeling lonely, would you like to change that? What can you do to meet some new people? I'm not going to pretend that making new friends is easy, because oftentimes, it's not. And it can take some time, too. But if you're willing to put yourself out there, you can make some new connections and see whom you might click with.

Can you join any clubs or apps or online groups? Or reach out to an old friend that you can get to know again? Or perhaps you can suggest to a friend that they invite one of theirs to your next hangout. What are some ways to take care of yourself socially?

While answering those questions, harness that balanced Libra energy, and remember that you deserve a life full of peace and harmony and to have loving relationships in your life.

LIBRA SEASON RITUAL

This Libra season ritual focuses on cultivating balance in your life, so you need a crystal or other object you can use to represent balance.

Begin by finding a quiet and comfortable space free of distractions. You can pick a space indoors or outdoors—whatever is most comfortable for you.

Sit or stand in a comfortable position with your feet firmly on the ground. Make sure you feel stable in your position.

Take a few deep breaths: inhale through your nose, hold for a few seconds, and exhale through your mouth. Repeat this a few times until you feel relaxed and centered.

Now visualize a bright, white light surrounding you, protecting you, and filling you with balance, harmony, and peace. See it expanding and radiating outward, enveloping you in a warm, healing glow.

Take a moment to reflect on areas in your life that may be out of balance, such as relationships, work, home, or anything else. Are you working too much and not taking time for self-care? Are your relationships feeling strained? Is your space too messy? Take note of these areas and notice them without judgment.

Next, set an intention to bring balance to these areas of your life. This could be making more time for self-care, setting boundaries in your relationships, or taking steps to make your surroundings more comfortable for you.

Now take the crystal or other object that represents balance to you. As you hold it in your hands, visualize balance and harmony flowing into your life. Imagine the object radiating positive energy and filling you with a sense of equilibrium and harmony.

Next, create a positive affirmation that aligns with your intention for balance in your life, and say it. If you can't think of anything, you can simply say something like, "I am balanced and at peace," or "I am open to receiving balance and harmony in my life."

Take a few more deep breaths, allowing the energy of balance to fill your body and mind. When you feel ready, close the ritual and carry the sense of balance and peace that you've cultivated with you as you move through your day.

LIBRA SEASON MEDITATION

Here's a basic loving-kindness meditation to connect with the relational and loving energy of Libra season:

Start by finding a quiet place free of distractions. Sit or lie down in a comfortable position and release any tension in your body.

Close your eyes and take a couple of deep breaths in through your nose and out through your mouth. Continue with the breaths until you feel even more relaxed in your body.

Next, think of someone you love—anyone who conjures up a positive emotion for you, someone who makes you smile when they come to mind. It can be someone from your past, present, or future; a public figure you admire; a furbaby . . . someone who brings you feelings of love.

Now imagine this person or animal of yours is standing in front of you. As you look at them, feel those feelings of love that you have for them. Feel the warmth, the acceptance, the joy.

As you continue to gaze at them, say the words, "May you be happy. May you be healthy. May you be safe. May you live with peace."

And then repeat the phrases: "May you be happy. May you be healthy. May you be safe. May you live with peace."

Now send those feelings of love to any other friends, family, animals, or notable figures that you admire—people who bring you joy. And say again the words, "May you be happy. May you be healthy. May you be safe. May you live with peace."

Then extend the love even further—to all beings everywhere, all creatures of our world. And say: "May you be happy. May you be healthy. May you be safe. May you live with peace."

Last, but certainly not least—actually, this is the most important of all—imagine that you are standing in front of yourself. Project the same kindness, compassion, and love that you just wished upon everyone *onto yourself.* Feel that love, feel that empathy, feel that warmth, and feel that joy.

Simmer on those sweet, fuzzy feelings for a moment, and then say the words, "May I be happy. May I be healthy. May I live with ease."

Take a deep breath, and repeat them again: "May I be happy. May I be healthy. May I live with ease."

After taking a couple more long breaths, open your eyes. Hold on to the love that you had for yourself and others during this practice. Embrace it and carry it with you.

Libra Season Affirmations

Here are some affirmations to connect to the energy of Libra season. If these affirmations don't resonate with you, feel free to adapt them to fit your needs while still channeling the balancing energy of Libra.

I am fair and balanced in all my relationships.

I seek out harmony and peace in my daily life.

I am balanced in both thought and action.

I am surrounded by beauty and harmony.

I am able to see both sides of a situation and make decisions that are fair and just.

I am able to communicate my needs and wants effectively in all my relationships.

I am open to new opportunities and experiences that bring balance and harmony to my life.

I radiate love and positivity, attracting positive and healthy relationships into my life.

Libra Season Journal Prompts

What does balance mean to me? How can I strive for balance in my relationships, work, and daily life?

How do I currently seek out harmony and peace in my life? Are there any areas where I can improve in this regard?

How are my relationships best serving my life?

How am I fostering connections with others?

What are some things I can do to fill my cup?

Libra Season Card Spread

This five-card tarot/oracle spread focuses on the energy of the sun in Libra. To do a card spread, shuffle the cards and fan them out in front of you, face down. Then pick five cards that you feel most drawn to and use them for reflection with the questions below.

1. How does the energy of Libra season impact me?

2. What insight can I get into what fairness means to me, and how I can apply it to my relationships and daily life?

3. How do I need to change how I approach partnerships and relationships in my life?

4. How can I improve my communication skills and foster deeper understanding and connection with others?

5. In what ways can I cultivate more harmony and balance in all aspects of my life?

Crystals for Libra Season

Rose quartz represents love, compassion, and emotional healing. It can foster feelings of love, self-love, and connection.

Clear quartz represents cleansing, clarity, and focus. It supports the cleansing of negative energies.

Lepidolite has calming and balancing properties. It can also help with cultivating inner peace.

Ametrine is a combination of amethyst and citrine. It promotes creativity, mental clarity, and spirituality. It can assist in stimulating creativity and connecting to your spiritual side.

Howlite has calming and soothing properties. It releases stress and promotes balance.

Herbs for Libra Season

Rose represents love and compassion. It can help with fostering these feelings toward ourselves and others.

Lemon promotes clarity and attention. As such, it can assist with focus.

Jasmine promotes peace, tranquility, and relaxation. It helps with relieving stress.

Honeysuckle is linked to harmony and balance. It can help with finding balance in daily life.

Lady's mantle is associated with comfort and healing. It supports the need for emotional peace and tranquility.

LIBRA CORRESPONDENCES

Planet: Venus. In astrology, Venus is the planet of love, beauty, harmony, values, and abundance. It is associated with the qualities of grace, charm, and diplomacy. This planet governs art and aesthetics as well as romance, partnerships, and relationships. Venus is about pleasure, comfort, and all of life's luxuries. Archetypes for the planet are the Lover, the Empress, and the Goddess. Venus expresses through Libra's desire for harmony, beauty, and love in their lives.

Color: Pink. Pink is a warm and compassionate color and is often linked to feelings of love, grace, and empathy as well as to nurturing and caring for others. It's associated with connection and reconnection in addition to romance, tenderness, sweetness, and hope.

Element: Air. The air element represents intelligence, communication, ideas, connection, knowledge, inquisitiveness, quick thinking, and adaptability. The air element can be a harmonizer and connector. It's associated with the mind. Air signs are articulate, friendly, and great conversationalists. They thrive on learning new things and absorbing information in all forms. Air signs get things moving, which is why they're also known as the "winds of change." They also can be visionaries and forward thinkers. We see the air element expressed through Libra in their connection, communication, and seeking of harmony.

Modality: Cardinal. In astrology, modalities show us how the signs operate and the role they play in the astrological calendar to help move us through the year. Cardinal signs initiate new seasons. Libra, as a cardinal sign, initiates partnerships and balance.

Symbol: The Scales. The Scales represent Libra's desire for balance, fairness, justice, and harmony in all things. They act as a reminder not to overdo it or "tip the scales" in any one direction. In addition, the scales of justice represent law and legal matters and having a strong sense of right and wrong and what is fair in the world.

House: Seventh House of Partnerships. The seventh house is the house of partnership, relationships, and personal needs, and it's ruled by Libra. This house represents partnership in its many forms: romantic partnership, friendship, or any serious agreement between (usually two) people. It's about looking at your relationship to another. It's also the house of legalities and contracts. The seventh house can give insight on your personal approach to relationships.

Polarity Sign: Aries. Aries and Libra are the relational axis in astrology; it looks at our relationship to ourselves and others. Aries is a fire sign and is known for passion, vigor, courage, tenacity, and an ability to take the lead. The air sign Libra is connected to the virtues of harmony, balance, and fairness, and it's known for charisma and diplomatic skills. Aries and Libra are complementary elements that balance and harmonize each other. While Libra offers grace and diplomacy, Aries gives passion and energy. Aries can teach us lessons on how to love ourselves, while Libra can teach us lessons on how to love others.

Tarot Card: Justice. The Justice card represents fairness, balance, truth, cause and effect, and the law. In addition, it stands for making an important choice and thinking through its consequences and long-term effect on you, as well as how it affects others. It's about accounting for actions, the search for truth and clarity in thought, and seeking balance in all decisions.

8

SCORPIO

We now move from the balanced, harmonious, and charming season of Libra to the transformative, mysterious, and powerful season of Scorpio. While Libra season is all about cultivating balance and harmony in our lives, Scorpio season is about diving into deeper waters by investigating our truths, claiming our power, and looking at our shadow sides with love and compassion.

There's no sign quite as intense as Scorpio, no sign quite as curious about uncovering life's mysteries and what makes others tick. And there's no sign as fiercely committed and loving—once their trust is earned.

Scorpio is the eighth sign of the zodiac, and it's a fixed sign. In the Northern Hemisphere, Scorpio season takes place during the heart of fall, making the sign a representation of the essence of autumn.

When Scorpio season rolls around, we continue to see transformation in the trees. The leaves are getting even more colorful and starting to fall to the ground. This is also "spooky season," with celebrations like Halloween,

Samhain, and Día de los Muertos, which are all associated with death. Big themes this time of year are death
and rebirth and pruning away things in our lives that no
longer serve us to make room for growth. Scorpio season
is all about the phoenix rising from the ashes (another
Scorpio symbol).

Scorpio is one of the most mysterious (and often
intimidating) astrology signs. Scorpios have quite the
reputation. They are alluring and private, and because
they don't show all their cards, they are often misunderstood. But Scorpios are very layered. They put their heart
and soul into everything they do. They're not about the
fluff and shallowness of life—they run deep, just like the
water sign that they are.

Scorpios are natural investigators, mental archeolo-
gists. They love to know how people operate. If you've
caught a Scorpio's attention, they want to know everything about you. They are great listeners, and people naturally want to open up to them. However, Scorpios are
guarded until you earn their trust. But once you've done
that, it's secured.

As mentioned, Scorpios are legendary for their intensity, their obsessiveness, and their passion. While they
share the traditional planetary ruler of Mars with Aries,
their warriorlike energy is more tactical. They're not here
just to win a battle; they're here to win the whole war.
And their battle is more internal—it's more processing,
more penetrative, and more patient. But when they have
their sights set on something, there's absolutely no way
to stop them. They are a force, rewriters of rules. They
will fight for people and ideas that they love.

Scorpios are famous for their stingers, but they also
have incredibly big hearts. They're great at confronting
their pain and using it for a purpose, at turning their

sorrow into inspiration and their failure into motivation. And throughout it all, they're working to uncover and confront life's deepest and most hidden truths. They love a good mystery.

Scorpio is also connected to spirituality and the occult. They have strong intuition and are incredibly perceptive. They're not afraid of confronting the "darker" things in life, and they're regenerative and resilient. Scorpios are survivors.

The sun is in Scorpio from around October 23rd to November 21st, and if you were born during Scorpio season, then Scorpio is your sun sign. Scorpio energy is powerful, determined, intense, mysterious, sexual, transformative, and empathetic. The archetypes associated with this sign are the Strategist, the Mystic, and the Investigator. Their key phrase is "I desire."

Their element is water, and I see two elemental symbols for Scorpio. The first is an iceberg, as they are powerful, immovable, broad, and only show what's on the surface. Another elemental symbol for them is a pond. Just as a pond can appear calm on the surface, they have powerful undercurrents and layers that are not visible to others. A pond can also be a sanctuary for all sorts of creatures to call home and the source for healing and growth.

Pond water can get murky. It can become polluted. But it can also be cleansed and purified. In the same way, Scorpios can purify themselves and others and protect people from the negative influences that threaten to pollute our world.

With their ruling house being the eighth house of transformation, Scorpios feel comfortable growing and changing; interestingly, this helps them feel aligned and grounded. Many Scorpios find themselves in careers that have to do with psychology and investigation, and in spiritual and healing fields. Scorpios want people to be happy, safe, and protected. They have a great deal of empathy toward people. They can feel the pain of others on the soul level, and they want to do something to make it better.

Like other water signs, Scorpios are incredibly creative. Since they tend to be private, creativity is a way for them to express their emotions and opinions. It can be an outlet for them, which is why Scorpios also tend to gravitate toward things like writing, art, acting, music, and so on.

And now it's my turn . . . my sun sign is Scorpio, and many of the traits and archetypes associated with the sign resonate with me. I am someone who has spent my entire life wanting to figure people out. I went to college for psychology, and I worked as a journalist. I studied astrology for over a decade. I write nonfiction to help others learn more about themselves, and I write fiction so I can create characters that are on a journey of self-discovery. Understanding humans and human nature has been a never-ending obsession of mine for as long as I can remember.

But I've also applied this obsession to myself. I like to know why I do the things I do. I like to look at the unfavorable sides of myself and figure out how I can change them. I like to evolve. And this is something that my best friend (also a Scorpio) and I have discussed a lot—this longing not to be stagnant, to transform, and always to be changing for the better. And I think that's the part of Scorpio that often gets missed—their deep desire for growth, to shed their skin, to emerge from their cocoons, and to rise from the ashes.

Scorpios also share a way of thinking that resonates with me. I am aware that death is inevitable, that everything and everyone has an expiration date. Nothing lasts forever. And that perspective drives my gratitude and appreciation for every moment. Scorpios are aware of those truths; it's one of the things that drives them. They don't shy away from the difficult things; they embrace them—and they enjoy the entire experience of life. Despite Scorpios being able to see life for what it is, they still like to enjoy it. They like to have a good time. Scorpios know that life is precious, that every breath is a gift, and they put their hearts and souls into every moment of it.

SCORPIO SEASON THEME

This season, we draw inspiration from Scorpio's symbol, the Scorpion. Scorpions are regenerative and powerful, and they lurk in the shadows, their domain.

So, with the regenerative energy in the air this time of year and the scorpion's ability to be comfortable in the shadows, the theme we focus on is self-reflection—and finding love and compassion for ourselves.

Growth begins with self-reflection. We cannot change, evolve, and transform without having self-awareness about what we need to let go of and work on. Self-reflection is about looking at yourself honestly. It's looking at the things you keep hidden and that you may not like about yourself, and finding love, compassion, and empathy for them. It's about looking at what you want to release and change, but doing so with understanding and giving yourself kindness, love, and empathy.

These parts of ourselves that we often keep hidden are also referred to as our "shadow" shelves. Looking at our shadow selves is a self-reflection technique for getting to know our "darker," more unconscious parts. It's a type of inner work that tries to make us aware of parts of ourselves that we've pushed down or denied—like negative emotions, fears, and past traumas. Doing this is also sometimes referred to as "shadow work," and we can also do this technique with a therapist and/or an energy healer.

The goal of reflecting on our shadow self is to bring these parts of ourselves into our conscious awareness and figure out how they affect our behavior and feelings so we can try to find peace with them. We can do this by writing in a journal, meditating, going to therapy, or using other types of self-reflection tools like tarot—and astrology, of course. We all have a shadow self, and if you look at yours with empathy instead of judgment, what you learn may surprise you. I like to think of shadow traits as parts of ourselves that need more love and compassion. As we dig up our darker parts through gentle but honest self-reflection, we have to tap into that compassion. If we don't know what needs to be pruned away, we cannot grow and flourish. In the process, we'll feel better about who we are, discover our true likes and dislikes, and get a clear and accurate picture of ourselves.

Self-reflection and looking at our shadow self is not easy. Healing is not linear. I want to be clear here: you *do not* have to dive into places that you're not ready to dive into. You don't have to unearth things that you would rather keep buried for now. Because, again, this process can be hard. So you can simply start the self-reflection process during Scorpio season by pulling some tarot cards and seeing how you feel, or even doing some light journaling and just a few minutes of self-reflection meditation. Move at a pace that works best for you.

My hope is that you come out of Scorpio season finding more love for all sides of yourself, and just like Scorpio, allow them to help you transform and step into your power.

SCORPIO SEASON RITUAL

This ritual focuses on self-reflection. You need a journal or piece of paper and, if you wish, a tarot or oracle deck if you want to pull some cards. You can set your space by lighting candles, burning incense, or using some crystals. Feel free to check the Correspondences section below for items that correspond to Scorpio season.

Find a comfortable and quiet place free of distractions. Sit in a comfortable position and take some deep breaths. Focus on your breath and release any tension in your body.

Think about a situation that you would like to reflect on. It could be a recent experience, a past experience, a personal struggle . . . whatever feels right for you.

Now close your eyes and visualize what you want to reflect on. Try to relive it as vividly as possible, and pay attention to your thoughts and emotions.

After visualizing the situation, ask yourself these questions: How am I attached to this situation? What was (or is) my role? Am I being honest about my feelings in the situation? What can I learn from it? Am I being kind and compassionate and loving to myself while I reflect on the situation? How can I use what I've learned to help me grow?

Write down your answers in a journal or on a piece of paper. After answering the questions, draw a tarot or oracle card, if you'd like, to see if you can get some insight into your journey.

When you're done, say the affirmation, "I am allowing myself to reflect and grow, and I am loving myself through the process." Close the ritual.

Remember, self-reflection is an ongoing process and can be challenging at times. So, do these practices while giving yourself a lot of grace, and move at a pace that works for you.

SCORPIO SEASON MEDITATION

Here's a meditation for Scorpio season called *cord cutting*. It's a ritual that helps to release unwanted energy and reestablish healthy energetic boundaries.

Start your cord-cutting meditation by finding a quiet place. Sit or lie down in a comfortable position, relax your shoulders, and release any tension in your body. Close your eyes and take a deep breath in through your nose and out through your mouth. Allow your body to relax even more.

Now think about a person, thing, or even a feeling that no longer serves your best interests—something you want to release and let go of. Whatever it is, imagine it before you, and pay attention to what sort of feelings arise. Do you feel angry? Sad? Anxious? Just notice those feelings, and focus on your breath.

Next, imagine a thick cord attaching you to the thing you want to release. What does the cord look like? Does it have a color? Is it attached at your waist, your head, your heart? Notice all the details, and think about how you are ready to detach from this cord, to release this energy.

After taking a few more deep breaths, move into visualizing cutting the cord. You can cut it with a knife or scissors, or even burn it with fire—whatever works best for you. When you're ready, imagine yourself cutting the cord. And when the cord falls to the ground, watch it disintegrate. As it fully disappears, it takes the negative energy that was attached to you with it.

Now whisper the words "I release you," as you watch that thing, that person, that feeling fade away into the distance. It is no longer attached to you or your energy. You have let it go. Take a few deep breaths, and when you're ready, open your eyes.

Letting go of things is not always easy, and for some, it can take a bit of time. So, feel free to use this meditation as often as you need.

Scorpio Season Affirmations

Here are some affirmations to connect to the energy of Scorpio season. If these affirmations don't resonate with you, feel free to adapt them to fit your needs while still channeling the powerful and transformative energy of Scorpio.

I am strong and capable.

I am powerful and a force to be reckoned with.

I embrace my power and use it wisely.

I trust in my ability to overcome any challenge.

I am open to growth and transformation.

I am worthy of love and respect.

I am in control of my own destiny.

I am at peace with who I am and what I have accomplished.

Scorpio Season Journal Prompts

How do I feel about my own personal power, and what are some ways I can embrace it?

What are some ways in which I can tap into my inner strength and confidence?

What are some areas of my life that I'd like to transform or improve?

What are some ways in which I can embrace growth and change in my life?

How can I let go of any limiting beliefs or doubts that may be holding me back?

Scorpio Season Card Spread

This five-card tarot/oracle spread focuses on the energy of the sun in Scorpio. To do a card spread, shuffle the cards and fan them out in front of you, face down. Then pick five cards that you feel most drawn to and use them for reflection with the questions below.

1. What card represents my theme for Scorpio season?

2. What is being renewed for me this season?

3. What thing can act as an inspiration to assist my personal transformation?

4. How can I embrace introspection during this time?

5. How can I step into my power this season?

Crystals for Scorpio Season

Black tourmaline has grounding, transformative, and protective properties. It assists in transformation and protecting energy.

Obsidian is a reflective stone and, as such, represents self-reflection. It can support introspection and self-discovery.

Bloodstone represents courage, tenacity, and resilience. With bloodstone, people often feel motivated to embrace their power.

Topaz represents passion, creativity, and tenacity. It helps you connect to your inner fire and drive.

Onyx is a grounding stone that helps with anchoring to the present moment. It can also help you become more mindful.

Herbs for Scorpio Season

Wormwood has cleansing and protecting properties. It can assist with protecting energy.

Patchouli has grounding and balancing properties. It can help you feel more peaceful and connected to the present.

Lavender promotes peace, relaxation, and clarity. It encourages feelings of calm.

Black pepper has stimulating and purifying properties. It helps with releasing and purifying energy.

Catnip is helpful for relaxation, calmness, and balance. You can use it to unwind—and it's also supposed to be lucky during Scorpio season.

SCORPIO CORRESPONDENCES

Planet: Mars. Mars is the traditional ruler of Scorpio, but Scorpio has a secondary planetary ruler in modern astrology: Pluto, the planet of transformation and rebirth. In astrology, you can use modern or traditional planetary rulers. Since I focus on traditional, let's look at Mars. Named after the Roman god of war, the planet is about energy, drive, action, passion, physical vigor, and sexuality. It's the planet of boldness and courage and is linked to the Warrior archetype. Mars is a symbol for our willingness to take initiative, pursue our objectives, and establish and uphold our personal limits. Mars can reveal information about a person's drive and ambition in a birth chart, and it can reveal their propensity for passion, conflict, and hostility. Since Mars is frequently seen as the planet of the fighter and warrior, its energy might be described as aggressive and determined. Fiery Mars is seen in Scorpio's intensity.

Color: Black. Black represents power, strength, refinement, and mystery. It's also linked to elegance and sophistication. Black is also associated with the cycle of death, life, and rebirth, and immortality. The color has protective properties against negative energies.

Element: Water. The water element is linked to the unconscious mind, emotions, creativity, imagination, and intuition. It symbolizes our connection to our inner selves as well as the spiritual world. Water signs are known for being extremely perceptive, inventive, creative, and connected to their inner world. They are also known for being incredibly empathetic and strong readers of energy. And just like water (we can't live without it), they nurture and cleanse the world around them and aid in new growth. Water also has a degree of mystery, vastness, and wonder to it (think of the ocean), and it's incredibly deep, which also corresponds with all water element signs. We see water expressed in Scorpio's depth, mystery, and powerful energy.

Modality: Fixed. In astrology, modalities show us how the signs operate and also the role they play in the astrological calendar to help move us through the year. Fixed signs help stabilize the season and are the pillar and essence of the season they are in. Scorpios, being a fixed sign, help to transform and improve the world around them.

Symbol: The Scorpion. The symbol for Scorpio is the Scorpion, which represents change, power, determination, and resolve. Scorpions are known for observing, protecting, and delivering a lethal sting—when provoked. And with their regenerative properties, scorpions are also a symbol for rebirth and death, which is why they are also linked to transformation. Scorpions are also known for adapting to new situations and surviving in hostile ones, which speaks to Scorpios' perseverance and strength.

House: Eighth House of Transformation. This house is about metamorphosis, transformation, mystery, and other people's resources and is ruled by Scorpio. It's also the house of death and rebirth. It's linked to the mysteries of the unconscious mind. Sex and taboos are also connected to this house. And in addition to giving us insight into how we can transform, the eighth house is about joint endeavors and joint financial matters, and it can give us insight into how we handle those dealings.

Polarity Sign: Taurus. Taurus and Scorpio are the growth axis in astrology. Scorpio is about what we need to let die to transform and grow, and Taurus is about how to flourish and blossom with all the new growth. They are both fixed signs. This axis is also about resources. Taurus is about personal resources, and Scorpio is about the resources of others. As an earth sign, Taurus is characterized by solidity, realism, and a sense of foundation. Taureans are known for their appreciation of the physical environment and their sensual pleasures. On the other hand, Scorpio is a water sign and is linked to traits like emotion, intuition, and metamorphosis. Scorpios are associated with intensity and passion, and they have an inquisitive, probing nature. These energies can work together to foster positive development and change. Taurus is about shaping things, while Scorpio is about shape-shifting things. Taurus can teach us lessons on growth, while Scorpio can teach us lessons on transformation.

Tarot Card: Death. The Death card is one of the most misunderstood in the tarot deck. Many fear it because they think it means literal death, but it does not. On the contrary, this card is one of the most positive to come up in a reading, as it represents change, rebirth, and the closing of one door to open another. Think of a caterpillar turning into a butterfly. It can mark the end of something that no longer serves you, allowing the possibility of something greater. It's all about transformation and letting the past die.

9

SAGITTARIUS

We now move from the transformative, mysterious, and powerful season of Scorpio to the adventurous, spontaneous, and philosophical season of Sagittarius. This season asks us to embrace life's adventures, see things through an optimistic lens, and live out our truths.

After embracing the regenerative side of Scorpio season and looking at the things in our lives that we need to let die and release, Sagittarius season offers a much-needed reprieve. This energy takes what has been released and purged during Scorpio and uses it as motivation to live our best lives, to seek and discover. If Scorpio is all about the transformation, Sagittarius is what we do after the transformation. And because of this, the energy of the season is jovial; it's a celebration of being *alive*.

Sagittarius is great at seeing everything in life as a new adventure, that there could be something new and exciting coming their way—that there's a silver lining and a lesson to learn. This sign believes in possibility and thrives on freedom, and it's constantly seeking the truth and wisdom in all things.

Sagittarians love newness—boredom is their worst enemy—and they're great at squashing their inhibitions when they want to and allowing themselves to have fun. They are the friend you want at a party or to take a road trip with. They have a beautifully spontaneous spirit. And they are great at seeing the bright side, even when times feel grim.

Sagittarius is a fire sign, and their elemental symbol is a candle—which brings illumination to a dark room. This speaks to their optimistic nature. When no one else can, a Sagittarius is able to spot a light at the end of the tunnel, even when it's just a mere flicker. Many of them go through life with the perspectives "good things come to me" and "everything will work out as it should."

They don't sweat the small stuff and don't like to dwell on what can weigh down or distort their energy; they'd just rather move forward. To them, life's too short to focus on people or situations that don't bring them joy.

And just as their symbol, the Archer, shoots arrows to the sky, Sagittarians are not afraid to shoot for the stars. If they have a dream, they will go for it, even if it seems unrealistic to some. It's no accident that some of the biggest pop stars—Britney Spears, Christina Aguilera, Miley Cyrus, Billie Eilish, Taylor Swift, Nicki Minaj, Tina Turner, and many more—all have Sagittarius as their sun sign. It's tenacious and bold, which is fitting for these excellent storytellers and entertainers.

Sagittarius is associated with luck and good fortune, as Jupiter is its planetary ruler. Jupiter does things in a big way and has a "go big or go home" vibe. And Sagittarius can definitely have a "big" energy—a boldness, a confidence, and a way of shifting the room's attention when they walk in.

Jupiter is also about wisdom, expansion, and bettering oneself. The key phrase for Sagittarius is "I seek." Whether they seek new adventures, new experiences, or learning new things, the experience of discovery is precious to them. A Sagittarius will easily hop on a plane at a moment's notice to go somewhere they've never been before, or sign up for a weeklong summit to listen to a speaker they like. They're down for any sort of new adventure, even if it's only a new adventure for the mind.

Sagittarius is the ninth sign of the zodiac and appears from November 22nd to around December 21st. If you were born during Sagittarius season, then Sagittarius is your sun sign. They are a mutable sign, making them flexible and adaptable, and in the Northern Hemisphere, they transition us from fall into winter.

This time of year in the Northern Hemisphere is truly stunning; it's the end of autumn in all its glory, when nature shows off and is beautiful as the last of the colorful leaves fall to the ground. It's the last hurrah before hibernation.

Sagittarius energy is optimistic, spontaneous, intellectual, honest, daring, philosophical, and adventurous. The archetypes associated with Sagittarius are the Adventurer, the Philosopher, and the Free Spirit. The Adventurer and the Free Spirit are a little better known than the Philosopher, but it's one of my favorite Sagittarius archetypes.

The philosophical side of Sagittarius is one I don't see celebrated enough, but it's such a core value. Yes, the sign is incredibly fun, joyful, and spontaneous, and Sagittarians are big adventures and explorers. But the quest for knowledge and wisdom is a huge part of who they are too. They like to ponder and dig deep into things.

But while Scorpio, the sign that precedes it, likes to dig into what makes people tick and why they are the way they are—the *who* and the *why*—Sagittarius is more focused on the *what:* What is my purpose? What is out there for me to discover? What can I glean from this experience? They are often very spiritual, which plays into their desire to better themselves. They often enjoy learning about and doing things to improve their well-being.

In addition, Sagittarius rules the ninth house of philosophy, which is about higher learning, spirituality, travel, publishing, and astrology. This is why, besides finding themselves in creative fields where they can express themselves freely, they also tend to gravitate toward teaching, writing, podcasting, and other professions where they can share their ideas on a broader scale.

Sagittarius is on a never-ending quest for truth, and they are also known for speaking it—a Sagittarius is not afraid to tell it like it is. For Sagittarius, getting to the bottom of the truth helps them in their journey of trying to figure out the "what" in life. This is something they share with Scorpio, the sign that comes before them.

My sun sign is Scorpio, but I've always related to Sagittarius energy. I have Venus in Sagittarius as my birth chart ruler (more on that in the Birth Charts section), and I was born at the cusp, or near the end of Scorpio season—just a couple of days before it turns to Sagittarius. Interestingly enough, most people think I'm a Sagittarius when they first meet me. It's not surprising, since I really resonate with the sign's optimism and ability to hope for the best.

From my perspective, the true lesson we can glean from Sagittarius is how to enjoy life. As I mentioned, this sign follows the death-and-rebirth theme of the season before it. If you experience a rebirth of any sort, you approach life in a completely different manner—you make the most of it, and you put more time into what brings you joy. And this is truly what Sagittarius energy is all about—the joy of life's experiences and being a light that can illuminate our path in the process.

SAGITTARIUS SEASON THEME

For the well-being theme during Sagittarius season, we draw inspiration from the sign's desire for expansion and novelty by trying a new adventure.

Doing something new is invaluable for our well-being. It might sound strange, but doing something new helps improve memory, mood, and even motivation. It also can stimulate creativity.

In addition, trying something new can improve how we perceive time. Have you noticed that as you get older, time seems to fly by so quickly? I believe this happens because as we age, we have fewer memorable events and new things occurring in our lives. Consider that when you were younger, you were trying and being exposed to new things and situations more frequently, so you perceived time as moving slower. So, by introducing novelty into our lives, we can actually slow down our perception of time. We can home in on that during Sagittarius season.

Seeking novelty during this time can be as subtle or as wild as you want it to be. It could be simply going to a different coffee shop, reading a new book, or walking on a new trail; maybe it's learning to crochet, taking a pottery class, or cooking a new recipe. Or it can be something bigger, like planning a road trip or vacation—anything that's a change to your normal routine.

I personally like to seek novelty in what I read and learn about. I get excited cracking open a new book or diving deep into a subject I want to learn more about. Just taking in that new story or information helps to fill my cup.

During Sagittarius season, you can seek novelty daily, every week, or just once. However you want to do it is up to you! There's absolutely no pressure—you make the rules here. You can approach this spontaneously (which is very Sagittarius), or you could have a bit of a plan and write down what new things you'd like to do. Sagittarius season is about having fun, so make this exciting and enjoy yourself!

SAGITTARIUS SEASON RITUAL

This ritual is great for focusing on the season's theme of seeking new adventure.

Find a quiet place and set your space (if you need a refresher, refer to the Appendix). If you would like to work with any crystals, herbs, or colors, check out the Sagittarius correspondences in this chapter.

Begin by taking a few deep breaths in through your nose and out through your mouth, and allow your body to release any tension it may be storing. Set an intention to seek some sort of new adventure in your life. You could go somewhere new, learn something new, or try a new activity. Write down the intention or just simmer on it. Be specific about what kind of new adventure you want to experience.

Now think about what you hope to gain from this new experience and how you would like to feel.

Visualize yourself making this new adventure happen. If it's traveling to a specific place, imagine the steps to get there. If it's signing up for a course you're excited about, imagine those steps. Visualize yourself successfully completing your adventure and achieving your desired outcome. Allow yourself to fully embrace the journey.

As you imagine this adventure of yours coming to fruition, feel all the emotions coming to the surface and notice them. Are you excited? Nervous? How do you feel as this adventure comes to pass? Noting this beforehand can give you some insight into whether you should move forward.

Next, take a step toward planning this adventure. Tap into the motivation you felt by visualizing it, even if you just open a web page to research how to make it happen.

When you're ready, take a couple more deep breaths and close the ritual with the affirmation, "I embrace new experiences in my life. I am open and excited to go on new adventures."

SAGITTARIUS SEASON MEDITATION

Here's a meditation to connect with the joyful energy that goes along with Sagittarius season:

For this, we'll tap into the Sagittarian desire for joy. Start by getting in a comfortable position, and close your eyes. Now, bring your attention to your breath going in and then out through your nose.

After sitting with your breath for a minute, once you're calm and relaxed in your body, think about a time in your life when you felt a lot of joy, a moment that brings a smile to your face. Your happy place, if you will. If you can't think of a memory that conjures up the feeling of joy, you can create an imaginary one for yourself.

Once you have this memory or story in your mind, immerse yourself in it. Feel those feelings of joy and allow them to resonate throughout your entire body, from your head all the way down to your toes. And while you're bathing in joy, continue to breathe in and out through your nose. Now think about how you can add more joy to your life with little things you can do to replicate this feeling.

When you're ready, open your eyes and repeat the following: "I am allowed to have my joy. I am worthy of living a life full of joy and peace." And carry that reminder with you—that you are allowed to always have your joy.

Sagittarius Season Affirmations

Here are some affirmations to connect to the energy of Sagittarius season. If these affirmations don't resonate with you, feel free to adapt them to fit your needs while still channeling the expansive and adventurous energy of Sagittarius.

I am seeking new things that support my well-being.

I am adventurous and open-minded.

I embrace new experiences and challenges.

I am confident and independent.

I trust in my own abilities and decisions.

I am optimistic about my present and my future.

I am generous and kind with others.

I seek knowledge and understanding about the world and myself.

Sagittarius Season Journal Prompts

What new experiences or challenges am I excited to explore during this season?

How can I embrace my independence and trust in my own abilities and decisions?

What am I grateful for right now in this season of life?

How can I share my time, talents, and resources with others and make a positive impact on the world around me?

Sagittarius Season Card Spread

This five-card tarot/oracle spread focuses on the energy of the sun in Sagittarius. To do a card spread, shuffle the cards and fan them out in front of you, face down. Then pick five cards that you feel most drawn to and use them for reflection with the questions below.

1. Which card represents my theme for Sagittarius season?

2. What can I use to inspire me to do new things?

3. How can I seek knowledge and understanding during this season?

4. How can I embrace more joy in my life?

5. What are some ways I can be inspired to be more adaptable or spontaneous?

Crystals for Sagittarius Season

Turquoise is linked to communication and creativity. It encourages innate inventiveness and curiosity as well as fearless self-expression.

Black onyx relates to security, stability, and grounding. It can give a sense of comfort and help with focus.

Fluorite is linked to mental clarity and concentration. It can support increased focus.

Yellow jasper has to do with optimism, joy, and prosperity. It can support in cultivating positivity and help to attract abundance.

Chrysocolla is linked to self-expression, communication, and balance. You can also use it to encourage serenity and inner calm.

Herbs for Sagittarius Season

Turmeric promotes protection and purification, and it wards off negative influences and unwanted energies.

Ashwagandha stands for balance, grounding, and harmony of the body and mind. It assists with cultivating peace and mindfulness.

Maca gives vitality and energy. It can encourage vigor and enhance energy levels.

Rhodiola promotes clarity, focus, and inner strength. It can assist in finding motivation and reaching personal goals.

Licorice brings positivity, love, and good communication. It can help with cultivating joy as well.

SAGITTARIUS CORRESPONDENCES

Planet: Jupiter. Jupiter is the planet of expansion, optimism, luck, and abundance. It's a positive planet, carrying good fortune and good energy. It's also about gratitude and finding joy. It's connected to bravery and open-mindedness as well as curiosity and the drive to explore, travel, and seek knowledge. Jupiter symbolizes compassion, kindness, generosity, wisdom, and spiritual and philosophical endeavors.

Color: Purple. This color is associated with spirituality, magic, positivity, and abundance. It's also linked to knowledge, dignity, mystery, and intuition. In addition, purple can stand for achievement, prosperity, and success and is also connected to royalty.

Element: Fire. Enthusiasm, warmth, zeal, inspiration, and leadership are all correlated with the fire element. Aries, Leo, and Sagittarius are fire signs in the zodiac and are characterized by their confidence, bravery, and independence. Fire signs are frequently associated with vigor, passion, and creativity. They can be motivated by their aspirations and goals and possess a strong spirit of exploration and adventure. Fire signs are known for having a strong sense of identity and an independent spirit. They are risk-takers and experimental by nature, and they bring their lively energy to any situation. Fire is a symbol of renewal and purification because it can burn away the old and make room for the new. Fire can bring light and warmth, which can be comforting and inspiring. It also can fuel others and help light one's path.

Modality: Mutable. In astrology, modalities show us how the signs operate and the role they play in the astrological calendar to help move us through the year. Mutable signs transition us to the next season. Sagittarius, being a mutable sign, lets go of what doesn't best serve and finds enthusiasm for the next thing.

Symbol: The Archer. The symbol for Sagittarius is the Archer, a half-man, half-horse centaur that represents their desire for freedom and also adventure, higher purpose, and prosperity. The Archer also symbolizes the independent, self-assured, and ambitious traits of Sagittarius and corresponds with a need for expansion and to explore, which could be a pursuit of wisdom and knowledge. The Archer also means this sign's ability to "shoot high" for whatever they want and to achieve goals.

House: Ninth House of Philosophy. The ninth house is the house of philosophy, spirituality, astrology, higher learning, and publishing and is ruled by Sagittarius. This house is also associated with heightened awareness and cultivating a more expansive outlook on life. It's about the quest for knowledge, wisdom, and insight, and also finding direction and purpose. Adventure is also connected to the ninth house, such as travel and experiencing new things.

Polarity Sign: Gemini. The Gemini-Sagittarius axis is that of knowledge. This polarity is about communication and philosophy, adaptability and adventure, and intellect and expansion. Sagittarius is linked to the desire for exploration and growth, while Gemini is linked to the capacity for thought and communication. Gemini is an air sign also known for intellect and flexibility. The Gemini talent for interpersonal connection makes them ideal leaders and mediators. Sagittarius is linked to expansion, exploration, and philosophy. They have intellectual and spiritual interests and often prefer professions that provide the freedom to voice their opinions. Gemini teaches us how to acquire knowledge, while Sagittarius teaches us what to do with it.

Tarot Card: Temperance. The Temperance card is about balance, harmony, peace, and higher learning. It reminds us to seek tranquility in life, to stabilize our energy, and find patience and moderation in all things. This card also represents the desire to avoid extremes or polarities in any situation, to find compromise and happy mediums, and to be open to opposing views. In addition, it represents being adaptable and flexible and cultivating mindfulness in all we do.

10

CAPRICORN

We now move from the adventurous, spontaneous, and philosophical season of Sagittarius to the ambitious, intentional, and traditional season of Capricorn.

After connecting with that fun, fiery, and adventure-seeking energy of Sagittarius season, Capricorn brings us down to earth a little bit. It helps to give us some perspective, to bring some discipline and focus, and to connect us to our traditions and routines and home in on what we want to pursue in our lives.

This doesn't mean Capricorns, or Capricorn season, are all work and no play. Capricorn energy is by no means boring. But it does mean that this time of year, it's great to connect with that ambitious energy. Capricorns aren't called the CEOs of the zodiac for nothing.

Capricorns were born to climb. There's no mountain too high, no terrain too rocky. If they have their heart set on something, if they have a goal, they will not stop until they reach it. When they want to get shit done, they will get shit done; their work ethic is infamous. They have a lot of grit.

Capricorns are the marathoners. They don't need to sprint toward their goals—they have endurance to make it for the long haul. When everyone else has tapped out of the race, Capricorn is still running. Capricorn's ruling planet is Saturn, and we see this in their discipline and desire to build things that last. But this sign is also exalted in the planet Mars.

When a planet is exalted in a sign, it means that its energy thrives there, that it's stronger and can express its higher potential. And while we see Mars expressed through Aries with its quick, warriorlike energy, and through Scorpio with its intensity and passion, we see it exalted through Capricorn with its willpower and motivation and its steady effort to achieve its goals.

Because of their unwavering focus, Capricorns can come across as cold and unemotional, but they're definitely not. I have a strong appreciation for Capricorn energy (it's my moon sign, after all), and I believe they are often misunderstood. They're not cold and emotionless; they just don't get caught up in trivial matters. And they don't show their heart or their cards to just anybody. That kind of trust has to be earned. But when they love you, they're incredibly dedicated and loyal. They're the person you want by your side during a crisis, and they'll often show up in a heartbeat when you call.

Capricorn rules the tenth house of career and legacy, and legacy is a theme for this sign. All Capricorns leave a legacy, of any size, one way or another. This could relate to a career, passing down a recipe or a tradition, a love for a certain piece of art, or instilling a particular value. They like to preserve things they see as important.

Capricorns are the final earth sign in the zodiac wheel, and their elemental symbol is a mountain. It represents their unmoving, steady nature; their strong, solid foundation; and their keen ability to climb any metaphorical mountain and get to the top. Capricorns are great at taking action and staying the course. They don't just dream about the things they want; they make a plan. And they sometimes approach things in life as if in a game of chess—studying and strategizing how they'll make the next move.

Capricorn is the tenth sign of the zodiac. Its dates are from roughly December 22nd to around January 19th, and if you were born during Capricorn season, then Capricorn is your sun sign. They are a cardinal sign, initiating winter in the Northern Hemisphere; the first day of Capricorn season is always the winter solstice. This brings forth a time in nature of solitude, bareness, and quiet contemplation.

In the Gregorian calendar, Capricorn season includes the New Year holiday. It's perfect, since it aligns with that Capricorn mindset of planning and setting intentions and goals, which many do at the beginning of the year.

Capricorn energy is patient, practical, ambitious, independent, persistent, caring, and reliable. Some archetypes associated with Capricorn are the Executive, the Ruler, and the Old Soul. Their key phrase is "I achieve." But just because success and achievement are a big part of the sign doesn't mean that all Capricorns have big aspirations. However, achieving and succeeding is something they all can tap into—if they want to.

I'm a Scorpio sun with a Capricorn moon. I had a good number of Capricorns in my life throughout my young adult years—which isn't surprising, considering that people often get along with those who have the same moon sign as their sun sign—and one of my best friends grow-ing up was a Capricorn. This girl was one of the hardest-working, grounded, and genuine people I've ever had the pleasure of knowing. I watched her achieve things that anyone in her circumstances would have found difficult. She approached life in an undramatic, matter-of-fact way; she also was very traditional at heart. She loved to learn and always had a wealth of information and wisdom to share, but also made a point to have a good time.

This is something often forgotten: Capricorns can be a lot of *fun*. They can party just as hard as they work. A Capricorn can be facing an important deadline, but you'd better believe they'll still make time to come to your house party and throw back some drinks with you, and stay after to make sure everything gets cleaned up too.

Capricorn also has a sensitive and intuitive side. This is seen in their symbol, the Sea-Goat. The top half of the creature is a horned goat, and the bottom half is a fish-tail. The horned goat represents the ability to navigate through rough terrain, and the fishtail represents the mystery, depth, and emotion that corresponds with water.

This displays how Capricorns are connected not only to the groundedness, strength, and stability of earth but also to the sensitivity and spirituality of water. And they can navigate the material earthly realm, as well as the spiritual and emotional realm, with ease.

A commonality they share with the sign that precedes them, Sagittarius, is the realization that life is short. But while Sagittarius takes this realization and says, "Life's short; I'll make the most of it," Capricorn's lens is more like, "Life's short; I'll get done what I want to get done."

Because, just like those mountains they can climb with great ease, Capricorn longs to create something solid and long-lasting. Whatever that looks like for them, you'd better believe they will make it happen.

CAPRICORN SEASON THEME

In Capricorn season, we draw inspiration from the sign's ability to put a plan in place and make things happen. Our theme is setting (or reevaluating) an intention.

The intention you focus on during this time can be as big or small as you want. It doesn't have to be work or career related; it can relate to a hobby or something to take better care of yourself. Whatever you want to set your intention about is completely up to you!

Setting intentions is a great tool for motivation and inspiration, mainly because it feels exciting and fresh. But what about setting new intentions is good for our well-being? Well, we take care of ourselves to feel our best and be our happiest. And setting an intention can help foster that.

The timing of when you set your intention is what works best for you. Since Capricorn season lines up with the New Year holiday in the Gregorian calendar, if that resonates with you, do it then. Or set your intention on the first day of Capricorn season, or the new moon during the season.

I personally don't set intentions on the New Year holiday; instead, I like to set intentions throughout the year on new moons. However, many astrologers, myself included, like to take the winter solstice, the first day of Capricorn season, to plant the seeds of intention for the next Gregorian calendar year ahead. It's a great day for this, energetically.

On the winter solstice, the light of the sun begins a new cycle, so the idea is to carry the seeds of intention that you plant that day through to the beginning of the next astrological year (Aries season) and watch them bloom.

But *when* you choose to set your intention during this season doesn't really matter. What *does* matter is that your intention aligns with you, that it means something, that it evokes an emotion. Because the more connected you feel to your intention, the more likely you are to see it through.

Follow our Capricorn season ritual directions below. Regardless of whether your intention be for a baby step or a huge leap, remind yourself that you're capable of doing anything. Because, just like for Capricorn energy, there's no "mountain" you can't climb to the top of.

CAPRICORN SEASON RITUAL

This intention-setting ritual is inspired by the energy of Capricorn season. As noted, you can do it anytime you'd like throughout the season—or anytime after it.

Start by setting your space (if you need a refresher, turn to the Appendix). If you'd like to work with any crystals, herbs, or colors, check out the Capricorn correspondences later in the chapter. Choose either a journal or a piece of paper for writing down your intention(s) during the ritual.

Begin by focusing on your breath: take some long breaths in through your nose, and breathe out through your nose. Repeat this a few times until you feel relaxed and connected to your body.

Now, think about what sort of intentions you want to formulate for your life. They can be big or small—whatever you want! Maybe you want to say no to things that no longer serve you, or yes to making more time for yourself. You may want to continue to work toward a dream of yours—or anything you want to do to enrich your life.

Now ask yourself, "What do I need in my life right now? How are my needs being met? How am I supporting my passions? In what ways can I show myself more support?"

When you're ready, write down your intention (or intentions) for this season. Then read your intentions out loud (which is great for solidifying them in your brain).

Now close your eyes and bring attention to your breath. Visualize yourself moving forward toward your intention, and notice what that feels like in your body. Sit with that feeling for a minute. Remember, it doesn't matter how long it takes for your intention to become reality. Also, give yourself permission to change your goal at any point in the future if you need to.

Take a few more long, slow breaths before opening your eyes. Carry your intention with you as you move through the season.

CAPRICORN SEASON MEDITATION

Here's a grounding meditation to connect with the earthy energy of Capricorn season:

Find a peaceful, cozy spot to sit or lie down in that is free of distractions. Take a few deep breaths in through your nose and out through your mouth. With each breath, allow your body to relax. Once you're more relaxed, close your eyes.

As you take your next breath, imagine that when you inhale, you're absorbing the earth's calming and stabilizing energy. And as you exhale, you're letting any tension or stress out of your body.

Next, move your attention to how your body feels as it touches the ground or your seat. Take note of things like the surface's pressure, the temperature, the comfort level, and just notice them without judgment. If any thoughts arise, just let them pass through.

Starting with your feet, bring awareness to each part of the body, all the way up to your head. And as you arrive at each section, just notice how it feels and continue to breathe. Again, if any thoughts come up, just allow them to flow through you.

Once you get all the way up to your head, take a few more deep breaths. As you exhale, visualize all the stress leaving your body. It's moving away like the wind while you're relaxed and anchored to the earth.

Breathe in and out deeply a few more times, and when you feel calm and grounded, slowly open your eyes. Pause, appreciate how you feel after this meditation, and carry that feeling with you throughout your day.

Capricorn Season Affirmations

Here are some affirmations to connect to the energy of Capricorn season. If these affirmations don't resonate with you, feel free to adapt them to fit your needs while still cultivating the disciplined energy of Capricorn.

I am capable of big things. There is no mountain I can't climb.

I am disciplined, focused, and driven.

I am successful in achieving any goal I set my mind to.

I am responsible and accountable for my actions.

I am practical, realistic, and grounded in my approach to life.

I am confident in my abilities and trust in my own judgment.

I am worthy of love, respect, and abundance in all areas of my life.

I am grateful for the opportunities and experiences that come my way.

Capricorn Season Journal Prompts

How am I honoring my intentions this season?

What am I doing to maintain a healthy work-life balance?

How can I stay practical and grounded in the face of challenges and obstacles?

What are some ways in which I can show dedication in my work, relationships, and personal growth?

What are my values, and how do they guide my decisions and actions in my personal and professional life?

Capricorn Season Card Spread

This five-card tarot/oracle spread focuses on the energy of the sun in Capricorn. To do a card spread, shuffle the cards and fan them out in front of you, face down. Then pick five cards that you feel most drawn to and use them for reflection with the questions below.

1. Which card represents my theme for Capricorn season?

2. What can inspire me to stay on task with my intentions?

3. How can I climb new heights in my life?

4. How can I take better care of myself?

5. What are some limiting beliefs I might need
   to overcome?

Crystals for Capricorn Season

Jade relates to abundance and prosperity and can help
with cultivating such a mindset.

Smoky quartz is for grounding and warding off
unwanted energies, and it can help protect from energy
that no longer serves you.

Hematite promotes attention, focus, and anchoring.
It's beneficial for maintaining discipline and commitment to goals.

Pyrite symbolizes riches, success, and abundance. It
can assist in realizing objectives and attracting wealth
and prosperity.

Snowflake obsidian represents balance and inner tranquility. It supports finding peace and harmony and
assists in stress relief.

Herbs for Capricorn Season

Pine promotes protection and purification. It can also
support your ability to stay rooted.

Oatstraw links with peace, relaxation, and clarity. It
can help with relieving stress.

Parsley brings prosperity and abundance. It can assist
you in reaching goals and attracting success.

Gotu kola promotes rest, healthy sleep, and reduced
tension. It can aid in achieving inner peace and deep
relaxation.

Yarrow defends against unwanted energies and therefore can help protect your own.

CAPRICORN CORRESPONDENCES

Planet: Saturn. Saturn is the planet of responsibility, discipline, determination, accountability, and lessons. It's known as the Great Teacher and the Timekeeper and is connected to lessons, difficulties, and personal development. It's also about the limitations and restrictions we place on ourselves. Saturn can sometimes get a bad rap in astrology because of its connection to learning tough life lessons, but think of it as the professor who just wants to help us better ourselves. Its intentions are good, though sometimes those truths may be hard to hear. Saturn expresses through Capricorn in their focused and pragmatic approach to life, their ability to work tirelessly to meet their goals, and their endurance in the face of life's hardships.

Color: Gray. The color gray represents sophistication, intelligence, and neutrality. It's also linked to dependability, duty, and reliability as well as wisdom and knowledge. In addition, gray is a cool and calming neutral color that can conjure up a sense of serenity and harmony.

Element: Earth. The earth element represents stability, growth, abundance, dependability, safety, and rootedness. It symbolizes the foundation upon which all other things are built and the essence of the physical and material realm. Earth signs are known as the builders of the zodiac. They cultivate things out of life. They are great at enacting a plan to get to where they want to go. They enjoy routine and security. And just like the earth, they are strong and prosperous. We see the earth element expressed through Capricorn in their practicality, tenacity, and strength.

Modality: Cardinal. In astrology, modalities show us how the signs operate and also the role they play in the astrological calendar to help move us through the year. Cardinal signs always initiate new seasons. Capricorn, a cardinal sign, initiates plans and long-term goals.

Symbol: The Sea-Goat. The symbol for Capricorn is the Sea-Goat, which is half horned goat (on the top), and half fishtail (on the bottom). The horned goat symbolizes the perseverance that goats have to climb any terrain and reach the top of any mountain. And the watery tail of the Sea-Goat symbolizes spirituality and consciousness, the capacity to adjust to shifting conditions, and persevering through challenging circumstances. The Sea-Goat symbol represents ambition, tenacity, hard work, and concentration and the Capricorn's ability to navigate both the material and emotional realms. This aligns with Capricorns' ambitious side as well as the desire many have to explore their spiritual side.

House: Tenth House of Career. The tenth house is the house of career, legacy, reputation, and achieving goals. It's also associated with the midheaven, the tenth house cusp in the birth chart, which is an expression of your public persona and career. The tenth house can provide insight on your career aspirations and guide you on what type of career may suit you best. It can also give insight into how you can best reach your goals.

Polarity Sign: Cancer. In astrology, Cancer and Capricorn are the foundation axis—that of home and career. Capricorn is about legacy, and Cancer is about roots. They are both cardinal signs. As a water sign, Cancer represents the emotional foundation of life and, being ruled by the moon, it's about nurturing our deepest desires and what we need to feel safe and comforted. It's also linked to compassion and empathy. On the other hand, Capricorn, an earth sign, represents responsibility, discipline, and legacy. Being ruled by Saturn, it relates to the lessons we learn to get where we want to be in life. These energies work together to balance our inner needs and exterior desires. Cancer can teach us lessons on how to feel, while Capricorn can teach us lessons on how to persist. Both signs are known for being incredibly resilient.

Tarot Card: The Devil. The Devil is one of the most misunderstood cards in the tarot deck. It doesn't represent an actual devil but symbolizes the feeling of being trapped and restricted. It aligns with Capricorn's planetary ruler, Saturn, which can also be about restriction. It's also about releasing fear and understanding how it might have impacted your life. This card can act as a reminder to look at what in your life might be unhealthy for your well-being and what steps you might need to take to change that.

11

AQUARIUS

We now move from the ambitious, intentional, and traditional season of Capricorn to the forward-thinking, nonconforming, and hopeful energy of Aquarius season. This is the season to embrace your uniqueness, think outside the box, and focus more on the bigger picture and the collective. Expand your mind, embrace your individuality, and let your true self shine. It's time to celebrate what makes you unique and to remember that you bring something special to this world. Stand out, take risks, fail, and try again—do it all, because it's just part of the journey.

It's not always easy to carve your own path, march to the beat of your own drum, think differently than everyone else, and not be afraid to embrace your uniqueness. These are things, however, that Aquarius is very good at.

While Capricorn, the sign that precedes it, is about building structures that last and leaving a legacy, Aquarius is about tearing down structures to build better ones for the collective. Capricorn climbs the mountains, and Aquarius wants to take things higher—up to space, if you will!—and go where no one has gone before. Aquarius is about the possibility of what *could be*.

In the Northern Hemisphere, Aquarius season begins in the heart of winter—from around January 20th to February 18th—and if you were born during Aquarius season, then your sun sign is Aquarius. They are a fixed sign, meaning they represent the essence of the season. This is seen in the solitude and stillness that goes along with the heart of winter: the pondering, the reflection, and the quiet. If Capricorn season is symbolized by the beginning of winter, the idea of storing up and working hard to get everything ready for hibernation, then Aquarius season *is* the hibernation. Think sitting by a fire with a pile of books so you can gather knowledge and later emerge with new ideas on how to improve the world around you.

Aquarius is the eleventh sign in the astrological calendar. By the time we get to Aquarius in the zodiac wheel, we've picked up some valuable lessons along the way, and this is why the symbol for Aquarius is the Water Bearer. It symbolizes them pouring the knowledge from everything they've learned out upon the world.

Despite the Aquarius symbol of the Water Bearer, they are *not* a water sign. They are in fact an air sign, and very much so, as they are deep thinkers and have a big focus on intellect and the mind. A huge cornerstone of the sign is their desire to gain understanding, to learn, and to acquire knowledge. Their elemental symbol is space, symbolizing possibilities, vastness, and the excitement of the unknown.

Many astrologers just love Aquarians, because they have a huge heart for humanitarianism, an incredibly open mind, and a passion to shake things up and do them differently. They love being unique and different from everybody else.

The last six signs of the zodiac zero in on how we relate to others, and Aquarius is all about the collective. Their focus tends to be on the group rather than the individual, looking at humanity as a whole, and thinking about the future for us all.

For example, let's say a street full of houses loses its electricity. Most would approach this problem by getting the lights back on as quickly as possible, but Aquarius would add another layer. It wouldn't be about just getting the lights on but looking at the structure altogether and, if needed, building a completely new structure that could function more efficiently.

They are the sign of the future, and as such, they don't get too caught up in living in the past; they're also not ones to experience regret. They believe everything is just part of the experience and that things are meant to be just as they are.

Aquariuses are known as the rebels of the zodiac. And with their visionary way of operating, they leave a mark on whatever they do. While they can appear unorthodox, some prominent people in history have been Aquariuses. To name a few: Rosa Parks, Jackie Robinson, Galileo Galilei, Mozart, Harriet Tubman, Bob Marley, and Susan B. Anthony.

With their broad interests, Aquariuses can find themselves in a variety of different fields—ones that are creative, forward-thinking, or inventive, or ones that involve teaching or social work. Many are also drawn to careers in technology and science—anything where they can express their ideas and not be too boxed in.

Aquarius energy is innovative, progressive, visionary, imaginative, chill, eccentric, altruistic, and open-
minded. Some archetypes associated with the sign are
the Visionary, the Rebel, and the Activist. Their key
phrase is "I know."

Like all fixed signs, they can have a tendency to be
strong in their beliefs. But their stubbornness is a little
different from that of the other fixed signs. They will
change their minds if you give them a good reason to,
if the argument is solid enough. But it has to be solid;
otherwise, they will stay stern in what they think. But
they don't always *have* to be right, especially if there's
new information that leads them to understand that
they're wrong.

The Visionary is one of my favorite archetypes for
the sign, because I believe it shows the Aquarian talent
of seeing things in a way that others aren't quite able
to. They can see the potential in a situation and how to
make things better—the bigger picture.

I've had a lot of Aquarius energy in my life. I have
family and friends who are Aquariuses, and my husband,
Brent, whom I've been with since college, is an Aquarius. There are many things I love about my partner, but
Aquarius attributes of his that stand out are his ability
to go his own way and his forward-thinking nature. He
looks at things through a broad lens and always looks at
the big picture. He's also incredibly open-minded. I can
talk to him about the most random thing, and he always
listens, considers it, and asks me more about it. He's truly
accepting and welcoming of all people, not judgmental
at all, and wants everyone around him to succeed.

This is another thing I love about Aquariuses—
they're quite accepting. It's why they tend to root for the

underdog. They want everyone to be included and for everyone to have a seat at the table, a chance to win, and to get their time to shine. This most likely stems from their knowledge that we're all just made up of stardust—all of the same things.

There's also a strong hopeful quality that goes along with this sign. We see this also in their corresponding tarot card, the Star. The Star card represents hope, optimism, inspiration, and that good things are coming and are on the horizon. This doesn't mean that all Aquariuses are optimists (some are, for sure!), but more that they believe hope is never lost and can always be restored. New life will always sprout after the cold of winter.

This is what the Water Bearer is all about: pouring that hope onto the world. Because when we have hope on our side, there's nothing we cannot do.

AQUARIUS SEASON THEME

For the well-being theme for Aquarius season, we draw inspiration from Aquariuses' desire for knowledge and focus on broadening our minds and our horizons.

Activities that expand my mind are good for my well-being and help me de-stress. I love to read, learn new things, and absorb all the information that I can. I would far rather spend my weekend cozy at home, reading a book or watching something thought-provoking and insightful, than go out for a night on the town. Truly, that's my idea of a party.

Broadening our minds is about doing things that inspire new ideas, expand our perspectives, and enlighten us. This can help to prevent mental decline, has a calming effect on our bodies, and improves our emotional intelligence. Reading in particular can help us become more empathetic and empowered. See, you're helping your health right now by reading this book (wink, wink!).

In addition to reading, things like listening to a podcast, watching a documentary, having an engaging conversation, taking a course, visiting a museum, and more can all be great for broadening your mind and your horizons. It's about getting you thinking by doing what nourishes and enriches you.

Here's an example. Maybe you watch a documentary about respecting and preserving nature, and it opens your eyes to something you never thought about before in regard to our environment. You now find yourself thinking differently about the topic and want to live more sustainably. And that decision, while it might feel small, can help us all in the long run.

Or, let's say you read something about the health benefits of meditation and spend some time meditating daily, even just for a little bit—and this inspires you to give more time to your personal healing and well-being.

Broadening your mind can have a domino effect in so many areas of life. It can help us all grow as individuals, which in turn ends up benefiting the collective. And Aquarius is all about that.

When Aquarius season rolls around, make it a point to broaden your mind. You can start small by making time for it once a week, or set aside time every day. Either way, all that truly matters is making time for yourself, free of distractions, so you can absorb whatever you're doing. Regardless of what you do, lean in to that Aquarian ability to approach things with an open mind. You'll be so glad you did.

AQUARIUS SEASON RITUAL

Here's a ritual to try during Aquarius season. It's a fairly simple practice that can help you connect to your thoughts a little more. If you'd like to use any herbs or crystals during this practice that align with Aquarius season, please refer to the correspondences in this chapter. And make sure to have a journal or piece of paper handy for the ritual.

Start by finding a quiet place and a comfortable position. Once you're feeling relaxed and ready, set a timer for 10 minutes. (You can take more or less time than that, but for the first time, 10 minutes is the sweet spot.)

When you're ready, start the timer. Close your eyes and bring attention to your breath: in and out through your nose. Just sit and continue to focus on your breath. There's no need to manipulate or force it. Just notice.

From now until the timer goes off, I want you to sit there, breathe through your nose, and allow your mind to just do what it wants. Let it wander. Let it daydream. Let it go wherever it needs to go. And while your thoughts are doing their thing, observe them without judgment. They're just thoughts. Nothing more.

Once your timer goes off, take a moment to think about whether anything came up and stuck with you. Was there anything that inspired you? Anything that maybe you need to release? I like to do this ritual when I'm creating (or feeling writer's block, in particular). It helps me to have breakthroughs.

Now, grab your piece of paper or journal and write down anything of note that came up for you. And if nothing came up, that's okay. Just write down that you took some time for yourself to do a ritual and think on how that makes you feel.

Take a moment to reflect on what you wrote down, and then take a few more breaths to close the ritual. You can return to this practice as often as you want during this season.

AQUARIUS SEASON MEDITATION

Here's a meditation to build authenticity and connect with Aquarius season energy:

Find a quiet location where you can be alone and free of any distractions. Begin by taking a few deep breaths in through your nose and out through your mouth. With each breath, relax your body and release any tension or stress.

If your eyes aren't already closed, close them now. Think about how you might be rejecting or concealing your authentic self. What fears, worries, or insecurities are preventing you from expressing yourself authentically?

Now, as you're thinking about this, do so without any judgment. Show yourself love and compassion for whatever you might feel. With your eyes still closed, imagine yourself writing down, on small pieces of paper, these things that might be holding you back from expressing yourself authentically.

As you imagine this action, feel what feelings, thoughts, or attachments you have regarding these things, again without any judgment.

Now, imagine yourself putting these bits of paper in a bowl and burning them. Watch as the smoke sweeps away the things that are holding you back. Alternatively, you could actually write the things down on paper and burn them with a real flame. (If you choose this route, please do so safely.) Repeat the affirmations "I am proud of who I am," "I am embracing my authentic self," and "I embrace my individuality and uniqueness."

Open your eyes gradually, return to the current moment, and take a little time to ground and center yourself with a few deep breaths before returning to your day.

Aquarius Season Affirmations

Here are some affirmations to connect to the energy of Aquarius season. If these affirmations don't resonate with you, feel free to adapt them to fit your needs while still channeling the unique energy of Aquarius.

I allow myself to embrace my uniqueness.

I have the capacity to think outside the box.

I am authentic, and I love every part of myself.

I seek out new experiences and perspectives.

I am a visionary and a pioneer in my life.

I am connected to the universe.

I am confident and self-assured, and I trust in my own abilities.

I am independent and free-spirited, and I trust my own path and journey.

Aquarius Season Journal Prompts

What energy am I putting out into the world?

What does being authentic and true to myself mean to me?

What are the fears, doubts, or insecurities that hold me back from being my authentic self?

How can I expand my mind during this season?

How can I continue to grow and evolve as a person, and stay true to myself at the same time?

Aquarius Season Card Spread

This five-card tarot/oracle spread focuses on the energy of the sun in Aquarius. To do a card spread, shuffle the cards and fan them out in front of you, face down. Then pick five cards that you feel most drawn to and use them for reflection with the questions below.

1. Which card represents my theme for Aquarius season?

2. What can inspire me during this season?

3. How can I connect more with my community?

4. How can I reconnect with my true, authentic self?

5. How can I find hope and renewal during this season?

Crystals for Aquarius Season

Amethyst has calming and relaxing properties and relates to self-discovery. It can help with spiritual development, connecting to inner peace, and with stress relief.

Lapis lazuli relates to spiritual and intuitive properties. It can help you get in touch with your higher self and intuition.

Shungite has grounding properties and can help with protection from unwanted energies.

Tourmalinated quartz represents clarity and focus. It helps with mental clarity and promotes concentration.

Lepidolite has calming and soothing properties. It helps with regulating emotions and reducing stress.

Herbs for Aquarius Season

Echinacea promotes spiritual growth, self-reflection, and insight, and it helps with connecting to intuition.

Ginkgo biloba relates to mental clarity and memory enhancement. With it, you can tap into inner wisdom and enhance your analytical mind.

Green tea can increase energy levels and alertness. It helps with productivity.

Marjoram has calming and soothing properties. It helps you cultivate peace and harmony in life.

Eucalyptus has clearing and relaxing properties. It assists you against feeling mentally drained or stagnant.

AQUARIUS CORRESPONDENCES

Planet: Saturn. Saturn is the traditional planetary ruler of Aquarius, though Aquarius has a secondary planetary ruler in modern astrology: Uranus, planet of rebellion and expanded consciousness. In contrast to astrologers who use modern planetary rulers, I use traditional, so let's look at Saturn. Saturn is the planet of responsibility, discipline, determination, accountability, and lessons. Known as the Great Teacher and the Timekeeper, it's connected to teachings, difficulties, and personal development. Saturn expresses through Aquarius in their desire to share their lessons, wisdom, and knowledge with others and in striving to tear down structures so they can fix them—which benefits the collective in the long haul.

Color: Blue. This color represents a flow of ideas, imagination, tranquility, meditation, and peace. Many use it to enhance relaxation and meditation, since it's a pleasant color connected to the vastness of the sky and the ocean. It's also linked to trust, responsibility, technology, and wisdom.

Element: Air. The air element represents intelligence, communication, and ideas, and it's connected with knowledge, inquisitiveness, quick thinking, and adaptability. Associated with the mind, the air element is a harmonizer and connector. Air signs are articulate, friendly, and great conversationalists. They thrive on learning new things and absorbing information in all forms. Air signs get things moving, which is why some call them the "winds of change." They also can be visionaries and forward thinkers. We see the air element expressed through Aquarius in their quest for knowledge and wisdom, their forward-thinking nature, and their desire to share their ideas.

Modality: Fixed. In astrology, modalities show us how the signs operate and also the role they play in the astrological calendar to help move us through the year. Fixed signs help stabilize the season and are the pillar and essence of the season they're in. Aquarius, being a fixed sign, helps to cultivate new ideas and improve the world around it.

Symbol: The Water Bearer. A person pouring water from a jug, the Water Bearer symbolizes the pouring of wisdom and lessons on the world. It dispenses knowledge and freedom and shares its forward-thinking vision with the collective, aligning with Aquarius's desire to do the same. It also represents communication, sharing, and the flow of ideas and information. The Water Bearer also symbolizes unconventionality, uniqueness, and defying the status quo, as well as Aquarians' altruistic nature and desire to improve the world.

House: Eleventh House of Ideals. Ruled by Aquarius, the eleventh house is the house of ideals, of the collective, and of humanity. This house is about dreaming of a better future and connecting with your community, as well as luck and good fortune. Humanitarianism is also connected to the eleventh house, as are social justice and activism. This house is also about social relations and the virtues of networking, teamwork, and collaboration.

Polarity Sign: Leo. Leo and Aquarius are the axis of expression. Leo is about self-expression, and Aquarius is about group expression. They are both fixed signs. Leo, a fire sign, is linked to imagination, individuality, and leadership. Aquarius, an air sign, is linked to creativity, uniqueness, and altruism. It also relates to the yearning for independence and intellectual curiosity. Together, the energies of Leo and Aquarius stand for a harmony between warmth and originality, self-expression, and freedom. In addition, both Leo and Aquarius have a strong desire to stand out and be different, and they are also both caring and generous. Leo can teach us lessons on how to love and accept ourselves, while Aquarius can teach us lessons on how to love and accept the collective.

Tarot Card: The Star. This card symbolizes inspiration, purpose, renewed hope, optimism, luck, and finding joy in all the moments. It acts as a reminder that good times are coming and that life is full of blessings—you just need to look for them. This card is also about growth and regeneration as well as independence, originality, and innovation. The Star card is very positive and hopeful, and it aligns with Aquarius's desire and hope for improving the world and spreading a message of inspiration.

12

PISCES

We now move from the forward-thinking, noncon-forming, and hopeful energy of Aquarius season to the imaginative, intuitive, and compassionate season of Pisces.

While Aquarius, the sign that precedes it, puts a big focus on the head with knowledge and intellect and envisioning a better future, Pisces keeps that visionary spirit but brings the emotion into it, directing things back to the heart.

Just as there's a beginning to all things, there's also an ending. Pisces season is the end of the astrological year, the twelfth and final sign in the zodiac calendar. The story goes that Pisces represents the culmination of the journey of the soul that began with Aries. And throughout the astrological year, they absorbed all the lessons and evolution of the signs that came before—all the joy, happiness, and wonder, and also all the sorrow and heartbreak and pain.

This is one reason why Pisces is notorious for being compassionate, in tune with emotions and intuition, and all things mystical and spiritual. It's often called the "sign of sorrow."

Pisces season acts as a reminder that just as there is sorrow in the world, there's also joy. The traditional planetary ruler of Pisces is Jupiter, the planet that also rules Sagittarius. Sagittarius has an "everything will work out" vibe, which Pisces shares, but for Pisces, it stems from their belief in belief. The key phrase for Pisces is even "I believe." This references their gift of believing that anything is possible, even when things seem incredibly impossible.

The sun is in Pisces from around February 19th to March 20th, and if you were born during Pisces season, then Pisces is your sun sign. Pisces is a mutable sign, and in the Northern Hemisphere, it transitions us from winter to spring. This represents taking us from death to life in a way that only Pisces can.

Pisces is a water sign, and its elemental symbol is the ocean—mysterious, deep, and at times unpredictable. Just as the ocean can be calm and quiet, it can also be rough and loud. And the truth is, we'll probably never know what lies beneath the sea, because it's so vast, and this is a great analogy for Pisces too, as they have a world of depth inside of them.

The symbol for this sign is two Fish swimming in opposite directions with a cord binding them together. This speaks to how versatile and adaptable Pisces can be and also to the constant pull that Pisces has between reality and fantasy, between the physical world and the spiritual world. But this pull they have in opposite directions is also a strength, as Pisces can be extremely creative and innovative.

In life, they tend to go with the flow and follow their own currents. And while Pisces may at times have their heads in the clouds, they wear their hearts on their sleeves. They tend to leave quite an impression on the lives they touch.

Many Pisces can find themselves in artistic fields such as music, art, poetry, and photography, but also in anything that requires innovation, like architecture and science, in addition to fields that involve helping others, like nursing, counseling, firefighting, and emergency response.

Pisces are the caretakers who will sit beside you and hold your hand through heartache. They're inventors with huge imaginations, the dreamers searching for something grander. And Pisces is the intuitive with an incredibly strong gut feeling. They're very empathetic; they are emotional sponges and brilliant readers of energy.

Pisces energy is compassionate, open-minded, kind, romantic, intuitive, idealistic, imaginative, and artistic. Some archetypes associated with Pisces are the Healer, the Psychic, the Artist, and the Dreamer.

The Dreamer is the archetype that I love for Pisces, because dreamers are what they truly are at their core. This doesn't mean that all Pisces have huge dreams that they're reaching to achieve. Some do, of course. What it does mean is that Pisces are in a constant state of dreaming, something that many of us could stand to do more of. This can look like dreaming of something big they want to accomplish, letting their imagination run wild while they listen to music, or staring at the sky and thinking about all the wonders and possibilities. Dreaming is a big part of the sign.

My grandfather, an inspiration to me who passed away a few years ago, had Pisces as his sun sign. He was

Mexican-American, and he was a dreamer, an innovator, and incredibly intuitive. He started a masonry construction business in Los Angeles that was successful despite challenges and obstacles. He was even inducted into the Masonry Hall of Fame for his work. Lots of doors closed in his face along the way, but he believed in his dream, so he found windows and opened them for himself.

Pisces rules over the twelfth house of dreams. Aries, the first sign of the zodiac, rules over the first house, which is all about the self. But Pisces, the final sign, rules over the final house—which is all about the soul. It's fitting that the last house in astrology, the one that marks an ending, brings the focus to the soul, to our spirituality and inner selves. Often, when we're coming to the end of a journey, we put things into perspective.

And that's what Pisces season really gives us: perspective. We come back to our joy in life, to the beauty and the magic. Because the thing is, despite all the wretchedness in this world, you are always allowed to have your joy. Your joy is your right.

And, let's be real—the human experience can be difficult at times. Life is full of challenges, and so many things are completely out of our control. But something great about Pisces is that even with their awareness of all the sorrow in the world, they have faith that things will get better. They will find the magic. They will find the gratitude. And this inspires me.

PISCES SEASON THEME

For the well-being theme for this season, we draw inspiration from Pisces' ruling planet, Jupiter. One of the things associated with Jupiter is cultivating gratitude.

Gratitude is like adding some sweetness to a sour entrée. It's a balancer, a reframer. We all have it at our disposal, and it doesn't cost anything. Gratitude is such an important part of caring for our well-being. While ideally we should practice gratitude consistently, it's a great thing to home in on at the end of the astrological year during Pisces season.

Gratitude is a choice. We choose to find gratitude in our lives. It's about noticing and appreciating what we have, things that we might take for granted on a daily basis, that we might not even think about too often— like air in our lungs, food and shelter, or a flower blooming outside.

Gratitude can help with processing trauma, working through relational issues, and releasing bitterness. It can reduce anxiety and stress. It can make us more resilient and more content, and bring us to the present moment. And it can help us change how we perceive a situation, which can be incredibly beneficial when going through a challenging time.

For example, when I was in my 20s and experiencing some health trauma, gratitude kept me afloat when I felt like I was sinking, when the walls around me were caving in.

One time in particular always stands out for me when I think about finding gratitude in a difficult time. An ambulance rushed me to the hospital, where I would later need emergency life-saving surgery. In the ambulance, I experienced excruciating pain—hands down, the worst pain I'd ever had in my life. I had to refocus my thoughts so I didn't go into shock. And where I directed my thoughts was toward gratitude.

I told myself that I was grateful to be in an ambulance, that I was grateful to have kind first responders beside me. I was grateful for the surgeon who would perform my complex procedure. Keeping my thoughts on gratitude helped pull me through that traumatic moment.

I try to practice gratitude daily, even if I just take a moment to briefly close my eyes and think of something that has made a huge difference in my life. Now that I've become so consistent with practicing gratitude, it's become a seamless part of my well-being routine.

There are so many ways to practice gratitude, but putting pen to paper is the most effective, and the more specific you get, the better. The specificity helps tie emotion to it, and emotion is what we remember. For example, instead of writing down, "I am grateful for the weather today," say, "I am grateful for the blue skies and comfortable temperature and the fact that I was able to take my dog for a walk outside." Getting more specific connects you to the feelings of gratitude, which can have a bigger impact.

But at the end of the day, how you choose to practice gratitude is completely up to you. You can write down what you're grateful for (and even put it on sticky notes), recite it aloud, do gratitude rituals and meditations, or pause for a quick moment during the day and just think of what you're grateful for. Just carve out some time to focus on gratitude in whatever way works best for you.

PISCES SEASON RITUAL

This gratitude meditation or ritual is great to practice during Pisces season, but you can practice it at any time throughout the year. You can also do it along with any other gratitude practices or well-being rituals that you already have in place.

To start this ritual, you can set your space if you'd like. For a refresher, please refer to the Appendix. As always, for crystals, colors, or herbs to go along with the ritual, find some listed later in this chapter.

Start this meditation by finding a comfortable place and position—indoors or outdoors, seated or lying down. Choose a place where you can take a little time for yourself and not be disturbed.

Close your eyes and bring attention to your breath going in and then out through your nose. Spend just a little time here, just watching your breath and grounding yourself to the present moment.

Then, as you're relaxed in that space, think of something you're grateful for. If you'd rather open your eyes and write things down, that works too.

Remember, there's nothing too big or too small that you can be grateful for. It can be anything at all—air in your lungs, the gift of being alive, your favorite person, or your furbaby. It can be a book you enjoyed recently or the cup of coffee you had before breakfast. Whatever it is, reflect on it for a moment. *Feel* those feelings of gratitude. Let them sink in, and let the warm feeling of appreciation flow through your body.

Now, bring your awareness to your heartbeat. Notice its natural rhythm. Just the fact that it's beating is a miracle in and of itself, isn't it? That alone is something to be grateful for.

Continue to focus on the rhythm of your heartbeat and feel gratitude with each beat. Then imagine that the feeling of gratefulness is pouring over you like warm water from a shower spout. Let it cover every inch of your body from your head all the way down to your toes.

Then, bring your attention back to your breath and sit with this feeling for a moment. Close your eyes and say to yourself, "I am grateful for all that I have, and I am embracing the good things in my life."

When you're ready, open your eyes. And carry that feeling of gratitude with you throughout the rest of your day.

PISCES SEASON MEDITATION

Here's a meditation to connect with the compassionate energy of Pisces:

Find a quiet place where you can sit or lie down comfortably, free of any distractions. Take a few deep breaths, nice and slowly, in through your nose and out through your mouth.

Now, continue to focus on your breath, noticing the sensation as you inhale and then as you exhale. Pay attention to how it feels as the breath enters and exits your body.

As you continue to breathe, think of someone for whom you'd like to cultivate some compassion. This can be someone you're on great terms with or you've had conflict with. It could be an acquaintance or someone well-known that you admire, or it could be a furbaby. It can be anyone you want to cultivate compassion for or send some compassion to.

As you visualize this person, notice how you feel. Does any tension arrive in your body? Do you feel relaxed? Does a smile stretch across your face? Whatever feelings arise, just notice them without judgment.

Now continue to visualize this person. Imagine that they're experiencing a little bit of sadness. Maybe they're having a not-so-great day, or maybe they're feeling a little off.

As you visualize them feeling this way, try to connect to their suffering. Feel how you imagine they are feeling.

Now repeat these phrases: "Just like me, this person experiences suffering. Just like me, this person desires happiness. Just like me, this person desires love. Just like me, this person is doing their best in this moment."

As you repeat these phrases, imagine sending waves of compassion and understanding toward this person, recognizing that they, like you, are deserving of love and compassion.

You can continue repeating the phrases and sending compassion for as long as you'd like to.

When you're ready, take a few deep breaths. Slowly open your eyes and return to the moment before you. Carry that feeling of compassion with you throughout your day.

Pisces Season Affirmations

Here are some affirmations to connect to the energy of Pisces season. If these affirmations don't resonate with you, feel free to adapt them to fit your needs while still channeling the magical energy of Pisces.

I allow myself to go with the flow, and I believe in myself.

I trust my intuition and let it guide me on my path.

I let my creativity flow freely.

I allow myself to feel my emotions fully, and I don't judge them.

I am compassionate and understanding toward myself.

I am compassionate and understanding toward others.

I am grateful for the beauty and magic in my life.

I am strong, resilient, and able to weather any storm that comes my way.

Pisces Season Journal Prompts

What are some ways this season that I can refill my cup after giving my energy?

How can I connect more with my intuition?

How can I tap into my creativity and let it flow freely?

How do I show compassion and understanding toward myself and others?

How do I embrace change and growth in my life?

What are the things in the world that inspire me and fill me with gratitude?

Pisces Season Card Spread

This five-card tarot/oracle spread focuses on the energy of the sun in Pisces. To do a card spread, shuffle the cards and fan them out in front of you, face down. Then pick five cards that you feel most drawn to and use them for reflection with the questions below.

1. Which card represents my theme for Pisces season?

2. What do I need to release during this time?

3. What do I need to embrace?

4. How can I trust my intuition?

5. What lesson does this card hold for the end of the astrological year?

Crystals for Pisces Season

Angelite enhances intuition and divination. It can help you tap into intuition and listen to your inner wisdom.

Selenite has cleansing properties and promotes good energy. It helps with removing unwanted energy and raising vibration.

Celestite promotes tranquility and harmony. It can assist in finding inner serenity and establishing more peace in life.

Apatite is associated with focus and motivation. It can help you home in on creativity and achieve clarity.

Rhodonite promotes balance and can assist your healing journey.

Herbs for Pisces Season

Marshmallow root promotes harmony, peace, and tranquility. It assists you in cultivating balance.

Damiana helps you connect to your passions, with dreamwork, and to enhance your intuition.

Holy basil has protective and purifying qualities. It can help with clearing the energy in your space as well as protecting you from unwanted energies.

Jasmine is linked to feelings of peace. It can help you cultivate more love and tranquility.

Calendula is connected to happiness and cultivating joy and gratitude.

PISCES CORRESPONDENCES

Planet: Jupiter. Jupiter is the traditional ruler of Pisces, while a secondary planetary ruler from modern astrology is Neptune, the planet of spirituality, creativity, intuition, and magic. Though some astrologers use modern planetary rulers, I use the traditional ones, so let's look at Jupiter. Jupiter is the planet of expansion, optimism, luck, and abundance. It's a positive planet that carries good fortune and good energy, and it's also about gratitude and finding joy. In addition, it's connected to bravery, optimism, and open-mindedness. The planet is linked with curiosity and the desire to explore new things as well as being driven to travel and seek knowledge. It's also about compassion, kindness, generosity, wisdom, and spiritual and philosophical endeavors. We see Jupiter expressing through Pisces in their hope and empathy, and in their belief that anything is possible.

Color: Aqua. The color aqua is associated with healing, rejuvenation, magic, and connecting with the subconscious. It represents imagination, intuition, creativity, and emotional depth. The color is associated with water and therefore the spiritual and mystical world, as well as the mystery of the unknown.

Element: Water. The water element is linked to the unconscious mind, emotions, creativity, imagination, and intuition. It symbolizes our connection to our inner selves as well as the spiritual world. Water signs are extremely perceptive, inventive, creative, and connected to their inner world. They are also incredibly empathetic and strong readers of energy. And just like water, they nurture and cleanse the world around them and aid new growth. Water also has a degree of mystery, vastness, and wonder to it, like the deep ocean. We see a watery nature expressed in Pisces' intuition, imagination, and vastness in their ability to feel.

Modality: Mutable. In astrology, modalities show us how the signs operate and also the role they play in the astrological calendar to help move us through the year. Mutable signs transition us to the next season from the one we're in. Pisces, a mutable sign, is connected with dreams and visions and has a free-flowing nature.

Symbol: The Two Fish. The symbol for Pisces is the two fish swimming in opposite directions bound by a cord that represents the division between fantasy and reality. These fish symbolize the dual nature of Pisces. Since Pisces is a mutable water sign, it's characterized by flexibility, adaptability, and the ability to go with the ebbs and flows of life. The fish are symbols of the spiritual realm, intuition, imagination, mystery, and the mystical aspects of life. All this aligns with Pisces' emotional and spiritual depth as well as their adaptable and flexible nature.

House: Twelfth House of Dreams. While the first house in astrology is all about the self, the final house, the twelfth, is all about the soul. It is connected to dreams, mystery, imagination, spirituality, the subconscious mind, and magic. It is also the house of endings. It's about the unconscious or hidden components of the self and the mystical aspects of life. The twelfth house can shed light on how we feed our soul and prioritize our inner selves, and how we need to nurture our deepest desires and dreams.

Polarity Sign: Virgo. Virgo and Pisces are the axis of healing. Virgo is about reminding us to take care of our physical and mental health, while Pisces is about caring for our spiritual health. They are both mutable signs. As an earth sign, Virgo has the qualities of practicality, patience, and skillfulness as well as well-being and health. Pisces, a water sign, displays creativity, spirituality, and empathy. It also relates to the subconscious mind and imagination. Virgo is the plan, while Pisces is the dream. Virgo is about the small picture, and Pisces is about the big one. These energies can work together to shift the focus to healing our mind, body, and spirit. Virgo can teach us the importance of anchoring ourselves and keeping our feet on the ground, while Pisces can teach us the importance of connecting to our higher selves.

Tarot Card: The Moon. This card symbolizes the subconscious, emotions, imagination, and intuition as well as self-care and rest. It can act as a reminder to listen to your intuition and let it be your guide, just as the moon's light can guide us through the darkness. In addition, the moon represents magic, mystery, and the unknown. Since it's about self-care and rest, it can be a well-being check-in to see if you're giving yourself the care, love, and reset you might need.

13

LUNAR CYCLES

We've gone through how tuning in to the astrological calendar can benefit your well-being. Now let's go over how connecting to the energy of the lunar cycle can harmonize your life on a more micro level.

Talking about the moon could be an entire book of its own, but here's a brief overview of how to connect with the lunar cycles for well-being, plus moon basics and rituals.

While the sun moves us through an entire year, the moon takes us through one month. It's its own little cosmic calendar. Connecting to the lunar cycle can give our lives a more natural rhythm and help us feel more grounded and connected to the energy of the universe.

Our ancestors lived in harmony with the moon. We evolved with it and were connected to it. Without calendars or clocks, our ancient ancestors used the moon cycle to keep track of time. They also used it to track fertility, the weather, and agricultural cycles, like optimal times to grow and harvest crops. Even sea creatures synchronize their biological clocks with the moon's light and phases. The moon is the subject of folklore, mysteries, and fantasies and the center of stories around the campfire.

I don't know about you, but whenever I look up at the moon, it always feels so magical—the way it glows in the dark sky and the way it provides us with light. And even on new moon days when I can't see it at all, just knowing it's there is comforting, in a way.

I like to track the phases of the moon and its sign placements on the daily. I've found that connecting to the natural rhythm of the universe has significantly improved my overall well-being. Each moon phase has its own special energy, and by attuning to it, I know that the new moon is a good time to set intentions. When the full moon arrives, it's a time for celebration and thinking about releasing things that no longer serve me. The waning crescent is nature's reminder for us to recuperate and rest.

The moon is the closest celestial body to Earth. It represents our nurturing, gentle, wise, and emotional energies and has always been connected to feminine energy. In addition, the moon is the "cosmic mother" in the sky.

But while the new moon and the full moon are the two big energy days of the lunar cycle, the moon has eight different phases: the new moon, waxing crescent, first quarter, waxing gibbous, full moon, waning gibbous, last quarter, and waning crescent. These are the phases that I recognize. Other cultures and belief systems use different phases, but these eight are the ones we'll use here.

In this section, you'll find rituals, tarot/oracle spreads, and affirmations for all phases, but you don't have to work with all of them every single month if that doesn't resonate with you.

How you want to use the lunar cycle is entirely up to you! You can do a more specific ritual on every phase if you'd like—whatever resonates.

Let's get started!

THE NEW MOON

The lunar cycle begins with the new moon. Think of it as a cosmic reset—a fresh start, a clean slate, a breath of fresh air. It's a blank canvas, a time to plant seeds for the cycle ahead. Like the full moon, the new moon is a big energy day in the lunar cycle, and it's the phase when we set intentions.

So, the new moon is a time for beginnings. Due to the moon's position between the earth and the sun, it's not visible in the sky, as it's at zero percent illumination. The new moon is a time for introspection due to the darkness in the sky, because the moon's lighted side is facing away from the earth.

The new moon is a sign of rebirth and renewal in many mystical and spiritual traditions. It's a time to let the past go and sow the seeds of our intentions and aspirations for the future. The new moon is a period of mystery, possibility, and change.

The moon's gravitational pull that causes tides to rise and fall is strong during the new moon, and it affects the moisture in the soil. This means that seeds absorb more water during the new moon, resulting in more growth. This is a great metaphor for our intentions. We plant the seeds on the new moon and allow them to grow throughout the lunar cycle.

NEW MOON RITUAL

For this new moon ritual, you need a piece of paper or journal to write down your intentions.

Start this ritual by finding a quiet and comfortable place where you can set your space. As always, for more details on setting your space, refer to the Appendix at the end of the book.

Next, clear the space of any unwanted energies to foster a fresh atmosphere. To do this, you can use a crystal, sound bowls, bells, or smudging herbs.

Spend some time grounding yourself by taking a few deep breaths in through your nose and out through your mouth. Once you feel calm and relaxed in your body, it's time to think about what kind of intentions you want to set for the upcoming lunar cycle.

These can be general goals for personal development, ways to prioritize your well-being, or any other objective or aspect of your life. Whatever you want to focus on for your intentions is completely up to you, and it can be as small or big as you want. Give yourself permission to start with baby steps. For example, if you want to set an intention around your well-being, you could choose to go for a 10-minute walk daily.

Once you're ready, write down your intentions on a piece of paper or in a journal or notebook. Now, take a moment to visualize your intentions coming to pass. Think about how it would feel to see them happen, and focus on the satisfying feelings and sensations that come up.

Repeat the following affirmations:

I am capable of amazing things.

I am attracting the kind of energy I want in my life.

I am worthy of living a life of peace.

Take a moment to give thanks for the new beginning and opportunities that the new moon brings before closing the ritual. Refer back to your written intentions throughout the entire lunar month.

New Moon Card Spread

This five-card tarot/oracle spread focuses on the energy of the new moon. To do a card spread, shuffle the cards and fan them out in front of you, face down. Then pick five cards that you feel most drawn to and use them for reflection with the questions below.

1. What blessings will this new moon bring into my life?

2. What energy or quality should I focus on in order to manifest my intentions?

3. What actions can I take to align myself with these intentions?

4. How can I best support myself during this lunar cycle?

5. What message does the new moon have for me?

New Moon Affirmations

I am the author of my story.

I welcome the new moon as a time of new beginnings and fresh starts.

I am open to receiving the positive energy and abundance of the new moon.

I am deserving of all the blessings and abundance that come my way during this lunar cycle.

I trust in my intuition to lead me toward my intentions.

WAXING CRESCENT

A metaphor I like for the waxing crescent is: just as the light of the moon is growing, the seeds of our intentions begin to grow within us too. The waxing crescent is the part of the lunar cycle when you take action around the intentions you've set. This is when the first sliver of light emerges following the dark sky of the new moon—when the moon is 0.1 to 49.9 percent illuminated.

The waxing crescent moon is the ideal time to begin moving toward your objectives, as this phase indicates a moment of possibility. It's time to let go of the past, concentrate on the present, and have faith that you can do whatever you set out to do.

Waxing Crescent Card Spread

This five-card tarot/oracle spread focuses on the energy of the waxing crescent moon. To do a card spread, shuffle the cards and fan them out in front of you, face down. Then pick five cards that you feel most drawn to and use them for reflection with the questions below.

1. What energy is present during this phase of the moon, and how can I work with it?

2. What area of my life should I focus on now?

3. What do I need to nurture and focus on in order to grow and see my intentions actualized?

4. What action should I take during this phase of the moon to move toward my intentions?

Waxing Crescent Affirmations

I am grateful and excited for the journey ahead.

I trust in my own strength and inner power.

I am focused and determined to move toward my intentions.

I am surrounded by positive energy and support.

I am capable of achieving all that I desire, and the waxing crescent moon is a powerful reminder to inspire me to do so.

I trust in the process of growth, and I am excited to see what the future holds.

FIRST QUARTER MOON

The metaphor I see with the first quarter moon is that the balance of light and darkness in the sky can act as a reminder that conflict is inevitable, but despite this, we have the power to keep moving forward.

The first quarter moon phase, also known as the half-moon, is the third phase of the cycle. The moon is 50 percent illuminated, giving it a half-circle appearance. This is a time for introspection and reflection, because the moon's light is getting stronger and brighter throughout the phase. It's a good time to review our objectives and make any required changes so we can move forward to support our intentions.

With the half-moon, the seeds of intention you planted are starting to take root. Growth is happening. This phase symbolizes commitment to moving forward despite any roadblocks we may encounter along the way.

First Quarter Card Spread

This five-card tarot/oracle spread focuses on the energy of the first quarter moon. To do a card spread, shuffle the cards and fan them out in front of you, face down. Then pick five cards that you feel most drawn to and use them for reflection with the questions below.

1. What challenges do I currently face?

2. What opportunities are available to me?

3. What can I do to overcome my challenges?

4. What can I do to take advantage of the opportunities available to me?

5. What should I focus on during this lunar phase?

First Quarter Affirmations

I am strong and capable of overcoming any obstacle in my path.

I embrace change and use it as an opportunity to grow.

I am confident in my ability to make the most of the opportunities presented to me.

I trust in the journey and have faith that everything is working out for my highest good.

I am grateful for the abundance and blessings in my life, and I welcome more of them into my experience.

WAXING GIBBOUS

The waxing gibbous is the fourth phase of the lunar cycle, when the light of the moon is starting to grow greater than the dark. The moon is 50.1 to 99.9 percent illuminated at this time, so it's more than halfway lit but not quite full. The waxing gibbous moon phase is for development, completion, and planning.

The moon's light continues to increase and intensify throughout this phase as we get ready for the full moon. You've planted the seeds of intention, the roots have taken hold, and now the buds are preparing to bloom.

In astrology, the sextile aspect, which stands for harmony, is connected to the waxing gibbous moon, so the energy around it is positive.

The waxing gibbous can rise at any moment between noon and sunset, and as a result, we frequently see it during the day.

Some have difficulty sleeping during this phase. If this is you, you might be sensitive to the moon cycles. Please get some extra rest and downtime.

Waxing Gibbous Card Spread

This five-card tarot/oracle spread focuses on the energy of the waxing gibbous moon. To do a card spread, shuffle the cards and fan them out in front of you, face down. Then pick five cards that you feel most drawn to and use them for reflection with the questions below.

1. What energies should I cultivate during this phase?

2. What progress have I made toward my intentions during this time?

3. What challenges do I still need to overcome to realize my intentions?

4. What can I do to overcome these obstacles or challenges?

5. What can I use to inspire me during this phase?

Waxing Gibbous Affirmations

I am moving closer to my goals every day, and I am grateful for the progress I have made so far.

I have faith in myself and my abilities, and I know that I can achieve anything I set my mind to.

I am aligned with my purpose and my passions.

I am confident and self-assured.

I radiate positive energy wherever I go.

FULL MOON

The fifth phase is the full moon, the peak of the lunar cycle. The full moon is associated with completion, fulfillment, and fruition. It's a time for celebrating our achievements and letting go of anything that no longer serves us.

The moon is full when it's 100 percent illuminated, which lasts only for a brief moment, but the full moon phase, and the energy associated with it, lasts longer than that. Like the new moon, the full moon is a high-energy phase, and the gravitational pull is at its strongest.

The full moon represents a balance of lunar and solar energy. It's always in the current zodiac sign's polarity sign, which symbolizes opposites coming together. For example, if we are in Aries season, the full moon is in Libra.

In addition to celebration and releasing things, the potent energy of the full moon makes it a great time to charge your crystals, make moon water (see page 44 for instructions), do moon circles, or write down something you want to release and burn it (safely). Or go for a walk under the full moon. These are all ways to connect with this magical energy in the sky.

Full Moon Ritual

Here's a ritual to connect with the energy of the full moon. You'll need a piece of paper and something to write with, a candle or something to burn the paper with (if you choose to burn it, please do this safely and monitor the flame), as well as whatever you would like to set your space with.

Start by setting up your altar or ritual space in whatever way works for you. Next, light a candle and close your eyes. Take a few deep breaths in through your nose and out through your mouth. Repeat this as many times as necessary until you feel relaxed in your body.

With your eyes still closed, take a moment to meditate on the energy of the full moon. Visualize its light and power shining brightly, and allow yourself to feel its energy.

When you're ready, open your eyes, grab your piece of paper, and write down what you would like to release. It can be one thing, or it can be a few things, but be specific about what you're letting go of.

Now, hold the piece of paper in your hand and visualize yourself releasing what you've written down. Imagine it leaving your body and your life, and feel the lightness and freedom of it no longer being a burden to you.

The next step is optional: to burn this piece of paper. If you do, please be mindful of fire safety and make sure to dispose of the ashes properly.

Using a candle, carefully light the corner of the paper and watch as it starts to burn away. As you're watching it burn, say, "I release what no longer serves me. I banish this unwanted energy from my life. I am free from this energy."

Once the paper is completely burned, take a few deep breaths. Close the ritual by expressing gratitude for the opportunity to release what no longer serves you.

Full Moon Card Spread

This five-card tarot/oracle spread focuses on the energy of the full moon. To do a card spread, shuffle the cards and fan them out in front of you, face down. Then pick five cards that you feel most drawn to and use them for reflection with the questions below.

1. What type of energy is the full moon bringing into my life?

2. What do I need to focus on most to grow and develop as a person?

3. What do I need to release from my life?

4. What deserves to be celebrated?

5. How can I best support my intentions for the remainder of the cycle?

Full Moon Affirmations

I am proud of how far I have come.
I am worth celebrating.
I am releasing the things that no longer serve me.
I am supporting myself and my growth.
My energy is bright and beautiful.

WANING GIBBOUS

The waning gibbous, also known as the disseminating moon, is the sixth phase of the lunar cycle. The waxing phases are the growing phases of the moon, while the waning phases are the ones where the light recedes. The moon is technically a waning gibbous when it's 99.9 to 50.1 percent illuminated.

The waning gibbous moon symbolizes closure, release, and letting go. It's a time of introspection and contemplation, as the moon's light is starting to dwindle at this stage. It's a time to get rid of the things that are holding us back and to create a way for what's to come.

The *trine aspect*, which is linked to the waning gibbous moon in astrology, signifies relaxation and comfort. In addition, the waning gibbous moon is a potent moment for connecting with our inner wisdom.

A theme surrounding the waning gibbous phase is gratitude. We have the theme of celebration on the full moon, and then the theme of gratitude during the phase to follow. This is a great time to be grateful for all things, but also to focus on gratitude for any growth or lessons you've learned along the way during this lunar cycle.

Waning Gibbous Card Spread

This five-card tarot/oracle spread focuses on the energy of the waning gibbous. To do a card spread, shuffle the cards and fan them out in front of you, face down. Then pick five cards that you feel most drawn to and use them for reflection with the questions below.

1. What can I let go of during this phase?

2. What is something I should put more gratitude toward?

3. What actions can I take to support my growth and development?

4. What do I need to focus more on?

5. What energy is this phase representing for me?

Waning Gibbous Affirmations

I am grateful for any progress I am making toward my intentions.

I am worthy of good things in my life.

I am committed to my growth and development.

I am worthy of happiness.

I trust my path.

LAST QUARTER

The last quarter waning moon, also known as the third quarter moon, is the seventh phase of the lunar cycle. Like the first quarter moon, this phase is 50 percent illuminated.

This phase is about release, cutting cords, and letting go. The moon's light is getting increasingly dim during this phase, making it ideal for introspection. It's time to make room for the new by letting go of the old. Since the new moon is quickly approaching, the last quarter moon is also a good time to wrap up any unfinished business.

When the moon is in its last quarter, it is in a *square aspect*, which in astrology indicates challenges that can present opportunities for growth and change. This phase is the time to take another look at what could be holding you back from moving forward or is getting in your way.

Last Quarter Card Spread

This five-card tarot/oracle spread focuses on the energy of the last quarter moon. To do a card spread, shuffle the cards and fan them out in front of you, face down. Then pick five cards that you feel most drawn to and use them for reflection with the questions below.

1. What do I need to let go of to move forward in my life?

2. What is holding me back from my full potential?

3. How can I release these blockages and limitations?

4. What new opportunities are waiting for me once I release these burdens?

5. What guidance can the last quarter moon offer me as I release and renew?

Last Quarter Affirmations

I trust in my inner wisdom to guide my actions.

I am free from past limitations and beliefs.

I am strong and resilient.

I am at peace with what has passed and remain hopeful for what is to come.

I trust in my ability to create what I desire.

WANING CRESCENT

The waning crescent is the final phase of the lunar cycle. The energy of this phase is about reflection, contemplation, and closure. It's an ideal time to focus on endings and to prepare for new beginnings. The theme surrounding this phase is retreating inward, rest, and recuperation. As the moon is becoming darker, it's time to rest, restore, surrender to where you are, and align yourself with calming energy.

The waning crescent is the last sliver of light in the sky before the moon goes completely dark for the new moon. During this phase, the moon goes from 49.9 to 0.1 percent illuminated.

For people who garden based on the phases of the moon, the waning crescent is a dry time, one in which to avoid sowing seeds. Before the process starts all over again, this is when to lighten your load and take it easy.

As the moonlight fades, it's normal to feel a little tired, low on energy, or want to sleep a little more. Nature is telling us it's okay to take a break and to slow down, and that we sometimes need to hide, just like the moon. And that even on the darkest nights, we can find peace.

Another thing to keep in mind during the waning crescent phase is that a fresh start is right around the corner. You're about to leave everything that happened in this phase behind and cycle into a new phase.

Waning Crescent Card Spread

This five-card tarot/oracle spread focuses on the energy of the waning crescent moon. To do a card spread, shuffle the cards and fan them out in front of you, face down. Then pick five cards that you feel most drawn to and use them for reflection with the questions below.

1. What areas of my life need more attention and self-care?

2. What self-limiting beliefs or patterns do I need to let go of?

3. What steps can I take to cultivate a more self-loving and empowering mindset?

4. What message does the waning crescent moon have for me regarding my self-growth journey?

5. What do I need to leave behind before this upcoming new beginning with the new moon?

Waning Crescent Affirmations

I release any negative energy that no longer serves me.
I invite positive energy into my life.
I embrace rest and relaxation for my well-being.
I listen to my inner wisdom and intuition.
I am at peace with where I am in my journey, and I trust that everything is unfolding as it should.

ECLIPSES

We can't talk about the moon's magic without mentioning eclipses. Unfortunately, they don't have the best reputation. Our ancient ancestors likely believed they were bad luck or even signaled danger or the end of the world. If you put yourself in their shoes, it's not as farfetched a belief as it sounds. Ancient societies depended on the sky for most everything that they did. They based their lives on the sun's and the moon's cycles and the seasons. Because eclipses were a big change from the usual, they were feared.

Now we know that eclipses just happen when the moon's orbit changes in a way that's a little more extreme than usual. Most years, there are anywhere from two to five eclipses, but some years can have as many as seven. A solar eclipse happens when there's a new moon, and a lunar eclipse happens on a full moon. During a lunar eclipse, there can also be a blood moon. While we know eclipses are not dangerous, many astrologers still think that eclipses are chaotic energy and not good times to do things like manifesting, charging crystals, making moon water, and so on.

I like to tackle eclipses a little differently. I don't view them as bad luck by any means. The energy that the moon gives off during an eclipse (like the gravitational pull and how it affects the tides) doesn't point to anything chaotic.

Second, I believe that when it comes to astrology, the stars are meant to *inspire* our lives, but they are not *in control* of our lives. We are the authors of our story. And I'm definitely not about fearmongering with astrology.

So, instead of being afraid of eclipses, I like to think of them as a reminder that life can sometimes diverge from the norm. And while change can sometimes be scary, we can also choose to accept it. Acceptance can be a very powerful thing.

All that said, if there's an eclipse on a new moon or full moon and you want to continue with your rituals and intention setting for that lunar cycle, go for it! Or if you don't feel comfortable, you can wait until eclipse season is over. The choice is yours. You can write whatever story you want to.

THE MOON AND THE ZODIAC SIGNS

Every lunar month, the moon travels through all twelve zodiac signs, making a full round every two to two and a half days. This is how we get moon signs.

And by tracking the sign that the moon is in, you can tap into a cosmic theme for that moon that can serve as a source of inspiration and motivation. So, for example, if the new moon is in Scorpio, the theme for that new moon is transformation. Knowing the theme, you can use it to help form the intentions you set on the new moon. And you can take it a step further: you can see what it's highlighting in your birth chart for transformation (more on that in the Birth Charts section). Of course, knowing the signs of the moon isn't required to work with the lunar cycles, and you don't have to alter your rituals with the themes. But knowing this information gives you the option.

Even though the sign the moon is in affects everyone's energy, you may feel especially in tune with the moon on days when it's in your sun sign or moon sign.

A moon phase calendar or moon phase app is the most reliable way to keep track of the current lunar phase and the astrological sign the moon is moving through. When you discover the sign that the moon phase is in, you can go to that sign's section in this book to get a handle on its energy. If you want, you can theme your rituals and also the crystals and colors you work with around the sign's energy too. Knowing the zodiac sign of the moon, then, gives us more ways to connect with the energy in the sky.

14

BIRTH CHARTS

We went through the energy of the zodiac wheel, a year around the sun, and looked at how we can connect with the astrological seasons to enhance our well-being. Then we went through the magic of connecting to the lunar cycle and learned how we can attune to the monthly rhythms in the sky. Now we're going to get personal. We'll look at the energy in our birth charts and explore how knowing our birth charts can level up our astrological journey. We all want to be seen, heard, validated, and loved, and understanding our birth charts is a great start.

Exploring birth charts could also be an entire book of its own, but here, we'll stick to the basics. I want to note that not all astrologers interpret the cosmic blueprint that is your birth chart the same way. One might read the language of the stars one way, and someone else might see something different. As always, take what resonates with you and leave what doesn't.

When I first started diving into astrology many moons ago, I had no idea what a birth chart was. Like so many others, I thought astrology was just about sun signs, because that's what the astrology books in the bookstore focused on. It wasn't until I started learning more that I realized that the sun sign was just the tip of the iceberg.

I discovered that in addition to being a Scorpio sun, I had a moon sign and rising sign, a birth chart ruler, and a bunch of other placements in my chart that gave me insight into energies and archetypes that I very much resonated with. I discovered that I had a stellium, which is when there are three or more planets in the same sign in a birth chart (more on what that means later in the chapter)—three stelliums, in fact! One in Scorpio, one in Sagittarius, and one in Capricorn. One stellium is in the eighth house and another in the ninth house, which points toward someone who would be drawn to things like astrology, psychology, music, and publishing. All are huge passions of mine. These are just a few things that I discovered through my birth chart. The insight I gleaned from studying my chart has been wild for me—in a good way—and incredibly affirming.

If you've been looking only at your sun sign, I'm here to convince you to go deeper. The truth is, with the sun sign, you've only scratched the surface on your own unique magic that goes along with the day you were born.

Interestingly enough, I've met people who are resistant to discovering their birth chart because they love their sun sign, so they don't want to know about any of the other placements. Trust me, I get it. But looking only at sun sign astrology is kind of like eating the frosting off the cupcake and throwing the cake away. Sure, you might be getting the best part (now you know where I stand on the icing-versus-cake debate), but you've left so much substance behind. And that's just what birth charts do—they add more substance to your sun sign and help it shine even brighter. They don't take away from it.

A birth chart, also known as a natal chart, is a snapshot of the sky at the exact moment that you were born, when you first entered this beautiful world and took your very first breath. And since we look at not just the birthday but also the birth time and location, this gives us millions and millions of possibilities. Think of your birth chart as your own cosmic blueprint of the energy that was in the sky at your moment of arrival. It's an energetic map you can use for inspiration, growth, and insight and a way to discover different parts of yourself, be seen, and love yourself on a deeper level.

While having your birth time is the best way to get the most possible accuracy in your chart, if you don't have your birth time, we can still work with that. In this case, you can do a sunrise chart.

For a sunrise chart, look up the time of the sunrise for the day and location of your birth. For example, search, "What was the sunrise time on March 22, 1995, in New York, New York," and then use that time as your birth time.

Once you have your birthday, birth time, and location, you can input your information into an online birth chart generator (some good sites for this are Cafe Astrology, Astro-Charts, and Astro-Seek), and start diving into what each placement means for you. Of course, if you really want to get a handle on it, it's best to get a reading with a trained astrologer. But you can absolutely start by getting information online!

As a reminder, the birth chart represents your energetic potentials and helps to confirm your intuition, but *you* are the author of your story. The birth chart is a cosmic guide that can inspire you, help you grow, and give you insight along your journey.

Let's start by going over the personal planets, also known as the inner planets, of the chart as well as your rising sign and chart ruler. These are the planets closer to Earth; they change astrology signs more frequently, which means they have a greater impact on our personal energy.

Sun Sign: The sun is a star, and it's also the star of your birth chart. It represents your identity and the primary energy you work with in life. It can give insight into how you shine and what you need to flourish.

Moon Sign: Your moon sign represents your inner self and emotional landscape. It's the part of you that isn't always revealed to others. It can give insight into what you need to feel supported and safe, and it also helps inform a self-care routine.

Mercury Sign: Mercury is the planet of information, so this placement in the birth chart is all about communication and how you process and share information. It can give insight into the ways in which you think and communicate, and also help you learn about your communication style.

Venus Sign: Venus represents the pleasures in life, love, beauty, abundance, and peace. This planet can give insight into what you desire and what you need to feel good in life.

Mars Sign: Mars represents drive, action, and how we assert ourselves and move things forward. It can give insight into how you take action and what you need to feel motivated.

Rising Sign: Your rising sign, also known as your ascendant, is the key that unlocks the birth chart. Without the rising sign, we don't know in which houses the signs fall in our birth chart. It helps set the tone of the chart's energy and also provides us with a birth chart ruler, which is an important placement to look at.

The Chart Ruler: In addition to the sun sign, the ruler of the birth chart is the placement that has the most influence, and we determine this based on the rising sign. Each sign is traditionally associated with a planet that is considered its ruler. For example, Pisces is traditionally ruled by Jupiter. So, if you have a Pisces rising and your Jupiter sign is Scorpio, your birth chart ruler would be Jupiter in Scorpio. That placement, then, is important as it represents the energetic theme of the birth chart.

To discover your chart ruler, take a look at this list of traditional planets and luminaries that rule your rising sign:

Mars: Aries, Scorpio
Venus: Taurus, Libra
Mercury: Gemini, Virgo
The Moon: Cancer
The Sun: Leo
Saturn: Capricorn, Aquarius
Jupiter: Sagittarius, Pisces

Outer Planets: In addition to the personal planets, rising sign, and chart ruler, we have the outer planets, also known as the generational planets. These are farther away from Earth and move more slowly through a given sign—anywhere from a year and a half to 31 years.

Jupiter Sign: Jupiter is a planet all about luck, good fortune, and believing that the impossible is possible. It represents philosophy, expansion, hope, and optimism. It moves through a new sign every 12 to 13 months.

Saturn Sign: Saturn represents order, duty, and discipline. It stands for challenges and maturity and can give insight into how we deal with those areas in our lives. It takes about two and a half years to move through a sign.

Uranus Sign: Uranus represents innovation, change, breakthroughs, and revolt. It is known as the Awakener. The planet takes about seven years to move through a sign.

Neptune: Neptune is linked to illusion, creativity, and spirituality. It can give insight into our natural connection to our spiritual side and our imagination. The planet takes about 13 and a half years to move through a sign.

Pluto Sign: Pluto is linked to rebirth, power, destruction, and transformation. It can give insight into what lies beneath the surface for metamorphosis, evolution, and discovering inner power. Pluto's orbit takes 248 years to complete, so this planet remains in each sign for years at a time, anywhere from 12 to 31 years.

Lilith: Black Moon Lilith (or Dark Moon Lilith, or just Lilith, depending on who's talking) represents untamed energy, a part of yourself that won't stay quiet. It's also associated with desires and liberation and how you can feel empowered. The planet takes about nine months to move through a sign.

POINTS AND NODES

In addition to planets, there are also points and nodes in the chart.

Midheaven (MC): The *midheaven* placement is one of my favorite points in the chart, and one that I consider incredibly important. The midheaven is the highest point in the sky at the time of birth. It represents career, public image, and legacy and can give insight into a career path.

Imum Coeli (IC): The lowest point in the sky at the moment of a person's birth is the *imum coeli*, sometimes referred to as the IC or *nadir*. It's situated below the midheaven on the opposite side of the chart. The imum coeli symbolizes a person's foundation and what's most significant to them, such as their roots, family, and home. Additionally, it might reveal a person's underlying traits and unconscious drives.

Descendant (DC): The *descendant*, also called "the seventh cusp," is the point on the birth chart that's the opposite of the ascendant, which is the point that represents the eastern horizon at the time of a person's birth. The descendant is the point that shows the western horizon and is at the start of the seventh house. This point shows how a person interacts with other people and with the rest of the world. As such, it is also linked to partnerships.

North and South Nodes: The moon's north and south nodes are celestial points that are linked to the moon's orbit around the earth. They are also known as "the points of destiny." They symbolize the areas of life where a person is naturally predisposed to grow, develop, and see changes.

Chiron: Chiron is an asteroid known as "the wounded healer." It represents wounds and how we overcome them, as well as where they might be able to help heal or guide others.

Houses: Your birth chart is divided into twelve astrology houses—sections in the sky—and each house represents something different. The twelve houses stand for many facets of life. There's a handful of different house systems, but I personally use what is known as the "whole sign" house system because it resonates with me the most.

Learning about the houses is where the birth chart starts to get really exciting, because understanding the house each sign is in gives you a little more insight into your placements. The houses are how astrologers cast horoscopes.

Each house represents a different part of life, such as love, work, personal growth, and so on. The twelve houses in astrology are made up of three groups of four: the *angular* houses, the *succedent* houses, and the *cadent* houses. The angular houses are the first, fourth, seventh, and tenth. They have to do with the person, the home, relationships, and the place of work. The succedent houses are the second, fifth, eighth, and eleventh. They have to do with money, creativity, change, and being part of a group. The cadent houses are the third, sixth, ninth, and twelfth. They have to do with service, learning, talking to people, and being spiritual. Looking at where the planets are in the houses can give you a better understanding of your chart and how their themes may relate to you.

For example, let's say your sun sign is Aquarius, and it's in the ninth house. The ninth house is ruled by the zodiac sign Sagittarius and the planet Jupiter. If you're an Aquarius with your sun in the ninth house, it indicates that you may thrive on adventure, travel, and philosophy. You'd likely enjoy pursuits like writing, while also having the open-minded, altruistic, and eccentric qualities of an Aquarius.

Let's dive into the houses.

First House: This is the house of self. It's a representation of you, including your likes, dislikes, self-interest, and vitality. It's ruled by the sign Aries and the planet Mars. It symbolizes your sense of identity, how you present yourself to others, and how you take action.

Second House: This is the house of abundance. It's about material things like money, belongings, and security. It's ruled by the sign Taurus and the planet Venus. It symbolizes the way we value ourselves and our worth, how we acquire, use, and manage our resources, and what we need to feel comfortable and stable.

Third House: This is the house of communication. It's also related to intelligence and information. It's ruled by the sign Gemini and the planet Mercury. It symbolizes how you perceive information and how you learn, speak, write, edit, think, and read. It also relates to analyzing and problem-solving.

Fourth House: This is the house of home. It's connected to how we nurture and how we want to be nurtured. It's ruled by the sign Cancer and the moon, and it symbolizes what we need to feel safe, stable, protected, and accepted. The fourth house is linked to our deepest emotions and needs.

Fifth House: This is the house of self-expression. It's connected to romance, self-expression, joy, and creativity. It's ruled by the sign Leo and the sun. It symbolizes a person's capacity for artistic, musical, literary, fashion, or other kinds of self-expression as well as playfulness. It also focuses on the things that foster happiness and joy in our lives.

Sixth House: This is the house of health. It's connected to well-being, daily routines, healing, and vitality. It's ruled by the sign Virgo and the planet Mercury. It symbolizes discipline, organization, and taking care of our body and mind. In addition, it relates to service to others and finding meaning and fulfillment in work.

Seventh House: This is the house of partnerships in all forms: romantic partnerships, friendships, or any serious agreement between people (usually two). It's ruled by the sign Libra and the planet Venus. It represents one person's relationship to another and can give insight on your personal approach to relationships.

Eighth House: This is the house of transformation. It symbolizes death and rebirth and is about metamorphosis, mystery, sex, and taboos. It's ruled by the sign Scorpio and the planets Mars and Pluto. It's also linked to joint endeavors and one's relationship with other people's resources.

Ninth House: This is the house of philosophy. It's about spirituality, astrology, higher learning, philosophy, and publishing. It's ruled by the sign Sagittarius and the planet Jupiter. It symbolizes the quest for knowledge, wisdom, and insight as well as finding a direction and purpose in life. Adventure and travel are also connected to this house.

Tenth House: This is the house of career. It's about legacy, reputation, work, and achieving goals. The tenth house is also associated with the midheaven placement. It's ruled by the sign Capricorn and the planet Saturn. It symbolizes ambition, tenacity, achievement, hard work, and our legacies.

Eleventh House: This is the house of ideals. It's about dreaming of a better future, connecting with your community, and humanitarianism as well as luck and good fortune. It's ruled by the sign Aquarius and the planets Saturn and Uranus. It symbolizes the collective, networking, idealism, collaboration, and humanity.

Twelfth House: This is the house of dreams, and it's about mystery, imagination, spirituality, the subconscious mind, and magic. It's also the house of endings. It's ruled by the sign Pisces and the planets Neptune and Jupiter. It symbolizes the unconscious or hidden components of the self, the mystical aspects of life, and our need to nurture our deepest desires.

THE BIRTH CHART'S DOMINANT ELEMENT

Discovering the dominant element in your chart is a great way to learn more about the primary elemental energy that you have in your chart. You can discover it by looking at all your placements and their elements and adding them together. I have five placements in earth signs, four in water, four in fire, and three in air. Therefore, the prominent element in my chart is earth.

Fire elements have energy that is passionate, warm, enthusiastic, and courageous. Earth element energy is stable, abundant, reliable, and grounded. Air elements have an energy that is intellectual, communicative, curious, and playful. Water element energy is intuitive, empathetic, artistic, and mysterious.

STELLIUM IN THE BIRTH CHART

A stellium is a cluster of three or more planets in the same zodiac sign or astrological house. Some astrologers count only personal placements (sun, moon, Mercury, Mars, Venus) for a stellium and leave out the generational placements. A stellium in your chart means its energy is stronger, and you're likely to resonate with that sign's or house's energy on a deeper level. It can also help to give insight into what makes you feel aligned and fulfilled.

BIRTH CHARTS FOR SYNCING WITH ASTROLOGICAL SEASONS AND THE LUNAR CYCLE

One of the coolest things about the birth chart is that it gives you the ability to use the astrological seasons and lunar cycle on a personal level. This is how you really get into what makes astrology so special and see how it can affect you as an individual.

Once you know the placements and houses in your birth chart, you can use them to look at astrological events for insight into how they might inspire you. For example, every month we have a full and new moon, and you can see where they're moving through (or transiting) in your birth chart to get a personal cosmic theme.

For example, let's say you have Virgo in the tenth house, and there's a new moon in Virgo. Your cosmic theme for this new moon could be centered around quintessential tenth house themes: your legacy and public persona. This would be a great time to set some intentions regarding your career, but also in a way that taps into Virgo energy—seeing if anything needs to be cleared, reorganized, or analyzed, or even checking in with yourself about whether you need more balance or grounding in that area of your life.

Virgo season is also a good time to launch something new careerwise, especially on the Virgo new moon. This is how a cosmic theme for an astrological season or lunar cycle can help focus what you reflect and work on during those times.

The above is just one example of how you can use your chart. Let's look at Beyoncé for another example. She appears to use astrology to launch projects based on what's going on in her birth chart. She once released an album on a Leo new moon, and then months later, she did one of her first performances in years on an Aquarius new moon. Leo and Aquarius are on an axis in astrology. Beyoncé has her north and south nodes on the Leo-Aquarius axis and has a Leo Mars (the planet of action). Many believed that she was ushering in a new era using this symbolism and that she used her birth chart as a tool for timing releases. Taylor Swift does this as well, releasing albums or songs on or near eclipses.

I've done things like this as well. I've released books during seasons fitting with my birth chart (including this one!). I've had projects release on full or new moons, and I launched my pop astrology brand during a season transiting my fifth house of creativity—and this was a new creative venture for me. I've chosen certain dates to set intentions around certain things. I've found a lot of inspiration, motivation, and personal success in doing this.

Your birth chart can be a great tool for planning and inspiration around all sorts of things in life. The best way to do this when you're first integrating astrology into your life is to work with an astrologer (this is one of my favorite things to go over with people in birth chart readings!). But continue to study your chart as much as you can, and get familiar with all the placements. Also get familiar with the transit and what's going on astrologically in the sky. But the better you understand your chart, the better you'll be able to understand how to align events.

BIRTH CHARTS FOR COMPATIBILITY

Compatibility is always a hot topic with astrology, as many like to look to the stars for love and relationship guidance. While people often just look at the sun sign for relationship compatibility, the entire birth chart can be incredibly insightful. This is a very rich topic. I just give you a snapshot here.

But I think one of the best ways to use the birth chart for love ties into self-care. Use it for insight into what *you* need in a relationship. For that, take a look at your Venus, sun, and moon signs. Venus, the planet of love, is a great placement to help you garner insight on how you love and how you like to be loved. The moon represents your inner self, so your moon sign can give you insight into what you need to feel safe in a relationship. And since the sun sign is our main energy and how we flourish, looking at your sun, moon, and Venus signs together can be very insightful. As people, we are multifaceted, and looking at these three different placements, to start, can offer mirrors for reflection into different areas of life that can help us discover what we might need in a partner.

Compatibility birth chart readings with a couple are some of the most enjoyable that I've done in my practice. But I always like to say, please take information on compatibility with a grain of salt. Any two people can make it work if they're committed to doing so, so I always advise people not to judge a relationship based solely on astrological compatibility. That said, the birth chart can be a fantastic tool for learning how to connect with your-self—and your partner—on a deeper level.

BOOKISH BIRTH CHART

If all of this feels like a lot—or if you just want a new way to view your chart—I have an analogy I like to use to help people understand mainly the sun, moon, rising, and chart ruler in their birth charts a little better: I view the birth chart through the lens of a book.

I've been using this bookish birth chart analogy for a long time now, but I've also heard astrologers use film, plays, art, and more. But for me, a lover of books, this one has always made the most sense.

Let's start with your chart as a whole. Your birth chart is the plot of your astrological story. It contains cosmic main characters, themes, personal worlds, and more that can reflect back to you, make you think, and open your mind—just like any good story does.

Your sun sign is the main character of your birth chart and astrological story. It's how you shine and how you flourish; it's the identity of the birth chart.

Your moon sign is the world in which the story of your birth chart is set. This is because your moon sign represents your inner self and your emotional landscape.

Your rising sign is the cover of the book of your astrological story, since the rising sign represents the first energy and sets the tone in your chart. In addition, the rising sign gives you your chart ruler, which is like the genre of the astrology story in your birth chart, or the energetic theme.

We can bring in some other planets: Venus would be the aesthetic of the story, the vibe, while Mercury would be the style in which it's written. Mars would be how the main character takes action, Jupiter would be how that character finds hope, and Saturn would be the lessons the character learns along the way.

Looking at your birth chart through the lens of a book can give you a second way of viewing and understanding your astrological story. For example, seeing your sun sign as the main character in your chart can help you tap into your sign's main character energy, to build your confidence and step into your personal power. Plus, the analogy is just a fun one and offers another way to help comprehend something as vast and complex as astrology.

CONCLUSION

While we've made it to the end of *Cosmic Care*, this is only the beginning of how you can use astrology to enhance your well-being. I hope that by now, you have a greater desire to take care of yourself and see how astrology, with its lunar cycles and birth charts, can play a role in your own personal growth, self-discovery, and self-support.

The ways in which astrology can support our well-being is a topic near and dear to my heart. I've watched it enhance my life in such a magical way, and I'm so grateful to get to share this with you.

Remember: everything in the book is just a cosmic guide. *You* are the magic. Astrology, lunar cycles, birth charts, meditations, rituals, tarot—all of these things are only tools to help you harness your own power.

You are more powerful than you know. You are capable of so many amazing things. And you are worthy of living a life full of joy, harmony, safety, and peace, and one full of so much love. I hope that with every day that passes, you find more love and acceptance for yourself.

But before we go, I want to leave you with this—a tarot card that I really love. I pulled it as a theme while working on this book: the Empress. The planetary ruler of the card is Venus (which happens to be my birth chart ruler), and its archetype is just what it sounds like—an empress. This is someone who knows their worth, nurtures themselves, and spreads love. This person lives in abundance and peace and makes time for what brings joy. The empress realizes the value in just being, in just existing, and finding the joy and love in that existence. That's what I believe our true purpose is . . . just to exist, and to enjoy our existence as much as we can.

And that's the energy I am sending to you: loving, abundant, peaceful, and joyful energy, and lots of it. Thank you so much for this great pleasure.

APPENDIX 1

EQUINOXES AND SOLSTICES

Here's a brief rundown of the equinoxes and solstices throughout the year and the representations and beautiful magic that each contains.

SPRING EQUINOX

The spring equinox refers to two moments in the year when the sun is above the equator with its rays angled perpendicular to the earth. Day and night are equal in length. It also refers to the two points in the sky where the sun's annual pathway and the celestial equator intersect.

In the Northern Hemisphere, the spring equinox occurs around March 20th or 21st, as the sun crosses the celestial equator heading northward as seen from the earth. In the Southern Hemisphere, the spring equinox occurs around September 22nd or 23rd, when the sun moves across the celestial equator southward. The spring equinox marks the start of spring.

With the energy of the sun gaining more area and sway over the earth again, life experiences a fresh start. The special, even magical nature of this equinox derives from the vast blooming of activity and vitality that occurs due to the earth's increased exposure to the sun's rays. Flowers, grass, and other new life multiplies, grows, and flourishes. Naturally, this pattern of fresh life has led humans to perceive the equinox as representing the regeneration of abundance, the outpouring of creative energy, and new beginnings.

Peoples throughout history have greeted the spring equinox with ritual and celebration to honor our connection with the sun as the source of our life energy.

Spring Equinox Card Spread and Journal Prompts

This five-card tarot/oracle spread focuses on the energy of the spring equinox. To do a card spread, shuffle the cards and fan them out in front of you, face down. Then pick five cards that you feel most drawn to and use them for reflection with the questions below. (Alternatively, you can use the questions as journal prompts for reflection instead, if you prefer.)

1. What new beginning or idea is being planted in my life during this time of renewal and growth?

2. How might I be available to nurture and support this new beginning or idea?

3. What can I do to bring more light and positive energy into my life to help myself thrive?

4. How can I best enjoy and appreciate this new season of growth?

5. What can I do to make the most of this new beginning and time for renewal?

SUMMER SOLSTICE

The summer solstice refers to the two moments in the year when the path of the sun is the farthest north in the Northern Hemisphere—around June 20th or 21st—or the farthest south in the Southern Hemisphere—around December 21st or 22nd. At the summer solstice, the sun travels the longest path through the sky, and the earth has its maximum inclination toward the sun. Owing to the long path of the sun and the earth's tilt toward it, the summer solstice has the longest period of daylight and the shortest night in the entire year. This event marks the official beginning of summer.

The deeper spiritual significance of the summer solstice comes from the intense exposure that the earth receives from the sun's rays that provide nourishment to life on Earth at that time—the ripe harvests, the abundance of both food and energy—all point toward a period of intimate union and close connection to the physical world, including nature and our own bodies.

Communion with natural reality is what defines the spirituality of the summer solstice. Honor of and connection with our bodies through movement, enjoying food in season, and connecting with others are how people have always celebrated the advent of summer represented in the solstice. Adhering to the natural rhythms of nature, people take time off during the summer to enjoy the fruits of their own harvest and revel in the physical world around them.

Even today, people around the world celebrate the summer solstice with a variety of festivals and traditions in honor of the sun's magnificence and power.

Summer Solstice Card Spread and Journal Prompts

This five-card tarot/oracle spread focuses on the energy of the summer solstice. To do a card spread, shuffle the cards and fan them out in front of you, face down. Then pick five cards that you feel most drawn to and use them for reflection with the questions below. (Alternatively, you can use the questions as journal prompts for reflection instead, if you prefer.)

1. What aspect of my life currently brings me joy?

2. What in my life am I holding back that could bring me joy, and what can I do to bring it into the light?

3. What passions or desires are stirring within me during this time?

4. What is something in my life worth celebrating right now (either big or small)?

5. What can I do to lean in to the positive energy of this time in nature?

FALL EQUINOX

The fall equinox refers to the two moments in the year when the sun is above the equator, making the day and night equal in length. It also refers to the two points in the sky where the sun's pathway intersects with the equator.

In the Northern Hemisphere, the fall equinox occurs around September 22nd or 23rd, when the sun crosses the equator northward. In the Southern Hemisphere, the fall equinox occurs on March 20th or 21st, when the sun moves southward across the equator. These events mark the start of autumn.

The fall equinox represents the end of summer as the sun's rays become more elusive, slinking further from life on Earth and ushering in more darkness and cold. Fall marks the end of the harvest season, when we take stock of what we've grown and gathered and give thanks for what we've received. This, along with the shift away from the radiance of the light to the coldness of the dark, makes the fall equinox the beginning of a period of introversion, solitude, and reflection.

The physical vitality of the summer fades into the intellectual pursuits and contemplations of fall. We turn away from the external, natural world and retreat inward, into the realm of the thinking self. Around the world to this day, people celebrate the spirit of the fall equinox by giving thanks for the summer months and paying tribute to the coming darkness of winter, building an altar with harvested produce and sharing food in a community. A variety of religious and cultural traditions around the world celebrate the fall equinox, honoring this beautiful time of year.

Fall Equinox Card Spread and Journal Prompts

This five-card tarot/oracle spread focuses on the energy of the fall equinox. To do a card spread, shuffle the cards and fan them out in front of you, face down. Then pick five cards that you feel most drawn to and use them for reflection with the questions below. (Alternatively, you can use the questions as journal prompts for reflection instead, if you prefer.)

1. How can I cultivate more harmony in my life?

2. What aspects of my life might need more balance?

3. What can I be grateful for during this time of abundance and prosperity?

4. What changes may be necessary to foster growth during this time of change?

5. What can I do to enter the next phase of my journey feeling renewed?

WINTER SOLSTICE

The winter solstice refers to the two moments during the year when the path of the sun in the sky is farthest south in the Northern Hemisphere, which occurs around December 21st or 22nd, and the farthest north in the Southern Hemisphere, which occurs around June 20th or 21st. At the winter solstice, the sun travels the shortest path through the sky, and the earth's poles reach their maximum inclination away from the sun, making it the day in the year with the least daylight and the longest night.

The winter solstice marks the pinnacle of the sun's hiding away from life on Earth, and it represents the momentary triumph of the darkness over the light. As everything lies silent and dormant on Earth, life recedes into a state of deep solitude. Quiet reflection is the birthing place of the light and the flowering of life; this reflective silence lays the seeds for new beginnings.

After the longest night and darkest day, the nights grow shorter and the days grow brighter until the summer solstice. Thus, the winter solstice represents the beginning of the gradual reintroduction of the light into the darkness, which is why some like to set their intentions for the coming year on the winter solstice. Cultures around the world have honored this moment with feasts and celebrations. Winter solstice celebrations vary across the globe and across history, but all express honor for winter and the coming light.

Winter Solstice Card Spread and Journal Prompts

This five-card tarot/oracle spread focuses on the energy of the winter solstice. To do a card spread, shuffle the cards and fan them out in front of you, face down. Then pick five cards that you feel most drawn to and use them for reflection with the questions below. (Alternatively, you can use the questions as journal prompts for reflection instead, if you prefer.)

1. What insights can I gain from taking time to reflect during this solstice?

2. What might be hiding in the darkness that I might need to explore?

3. What may I need to release during this time of rest?

4. What benefit might come during this time of hibernation?

5. What can I do to honor and celebrate my growth and progress?

HOW TO SET THE ENERGY IN YOUR SPACE

Resetting the energy in your space is great to do before a ritual, meditation, laying out a tarot/oracle spread, or any other spiritual practice. You can also do this whenever you feel like the energy in your space could use a reset. The process signifies letting go of old energy and welcoming in new, fresh energy.

You can always research the traditions of your own ancestral culture and see if any of its practices and rituals resonate with you. Connecting with your roots can be rewarding and make you feel even more connected to a ritual or practice.

For example, over the last few years, I studied the rituals and practices of my paternal grandfather and maternal grandfather's ancestral lines. Both passed away in the same year a few years ago, and for me, learning about their ancestral lines and practicing rituals from their cultures is a way to honor them.

My paternal grandfather's heritage is from Jalisco, Mexico, and my maternal grandfather's heritage is from Casablanca, Morocco, North Africa. This is why I personally like to reset my space with selenite from Morocco and black obsidian from Mexico, among other things. And knowing these things are connected to my ancestors makes me feel even more connected to the practice.

An important note: if you choose to do a practice from a culture that isn't your own, research it to see if it's a closed practice (meaning that it's meant for members of that culture exclusively). If it's not closed, find out how to practice in a way that honors and respects that culture.

I also want to note that resetting the energy in your space is about the mindful act of doing so. Whether or not a particular practice does what it sets out to do doesn't really matter. To our brain, it's just about giving us the feeling of control over a situation. So the act of resetting your space is what it's really about, regardless of how you choose to do it.

Here are some different ways to reset the energy in your space. You can do one of them, you can do all of them, or you can research other ways to reset your space and find one that resonates best with you.

Smoke or incense cleansing is a way to clean and purify a space by burning herbs like cedar, bay, or rosemary. You let the smoke rise into the air and fill the room to cleanse the energy.

Sound therapy can reset your space with sound. You can use singing bowls, chimes, bells, or a tuning fork to create vibrations that can reset the energy and clear the space.

Crystals are another great way to reset the energy in your space. Bringing crystals like selenite, black tourmaline, black obsidian, and clear quartz in, and taking some deep, clearing breaths, can help reset and balance the energy.

Plants in your space reset its energy. Bamboo, lavender, aloe vera, and peace lily, among many others, can help clean the air and bring in new energy.

Misting may seem simple, but try misting salt water into the air. You can add calming herbs to the spray as well, such as lavender, basil, and thyme.

Visualizing new energy in your space can reset it. For this, close your eyes and imagine a bright white light encircling your space, cleaning it and getting rid of any unwanted energy.

Opening windows or a door to the outside world is an easy way to reset. Just letting fresh air in can help bring new energy into a space.

ACKNOWLEDGMENTS

As with all books, a lot of love and support went into *Cosmic Care*.

To my editor, Anna Cooperberg, thank you so much for believing in *Cosmic Care* and being such an incredible joy to work with. You have such a beautiful, warm energy and I just have so much gratitude for the opportunity to work with you. Thank you for being so lovely!

To my agent Louise Fury, one of my favorite and fiercest Cancers, thank you for always believing in me and my work and for always being in my corner! I am so grateful for you, and I appreciate you so much.

To my family, friends, the writing community, the astrology community, and creator community, thank you for always showing me so much love and being so supportive of my work. It truly means the world.

To my partner, Brent, human sunshine (Aquarius with a Leo moon), thank you for always being my biggest fan and encouraging me to pursue the things that I love. To my dearest friend, Jessica, a true triple Scorpio queen, thank you for always cheering me on and for being a listening ear.

And to the entire team at Hay House, the creative team, copy editors, designers, marketers, audiobook producers, and many more, thank you so much for all the love and support for this book. I truly feel so grateful that *Cosmic Care* found a home here!

ABOUT THE AUTHOR

Valerie Tejeda is a best-selling author and astrologer with a B.A. in psychology and certificates in astrology and music therapy. In addition to novels, she writes nonfiction books about astrology and well-being. Her titles include the Audible Originals *Self Care by the Signs* and *Self Care by the Moon*, the novel *Good on Paper*, and more. Valerie's bylines have appeared in publications such as *Self, Vanity Fair, MTV, Teen Vogue, Latina, Marie Claire, Cosmo*, and more. She is the creator of the pop astrology digital brand Big Cosmic Energy. Valerie is a Californian who loves iced coffee, walking on trails, and asking people, "When's your birthday?" when she first meets them. You can find her at **valerietejeda.com** and on Instagram **@valerietejeda** and **@bigcosmicenergy**.